I'M GLAD YOU ASKED ME THAT

Irish Political Quotations

Eoghan Corry

HODDER
HEADLINE
IRELAND

Copyright © 2007 Eoghan Corry

First published in 2007 by Hodder Headline Ireland

The right of Eoghan Corry to be identified as the Author of this
Work has been asserted by him in accordance with the Copyright,
Designs and Patents Act 1988.

1

A CIP catalogue record for this title is available from
the British Library.

ISBN 978 0340 92452 5

Typeset in Berling Antiqua and Schindler by Hodder Headline
Ireland
Printed and bound in Great Britain by Clays Ltd, St Ives plc.

Hodder Headline Ireland
8 Castlecourt Centre
Castleknock
Dublin 15
Ireland
www.hhireland.ie

A division of Hachette Livre UK Ltd
338 Euston Road
London NW1 3BH

For Ida

And in memory of Larry and Donal Campbell of
Dromellihy, who witnessed so much history at first hand
and gave me my introduction to political theory

Contents

Contents

Introduction

'The only reason to give a speech is to change the world,' so said the most successful Irish politician of all, John Fitzgerald Kennedy. Unfortunately, they did not listen to him.

Politicians would like all their speeches to be like Kennedy's, visionary and memorable, fine words to be cut into the plinth when we erect statues to their memory on O'Connell Street. The rest of us know only too well that their finest words are more likely to be used for wrapping cod.

True, some of their great phrases have been cherished and remembered. Some are filled with martial grandeur, Ulster fighting and being right, Ireland striking for her freedom, severing the connection with England and not having boundaries put on the march of a nation.

Then there are those eccentric, vision mission statements about dancing at the crossroads, or who looks bigger than they actually are when the viewer is on his knees. And occasional economic erudition about rising tides lifting all boats, and Celtic tigers stalking the country. But the key to following politics is to understand that, like footballers, politicians rarely say anything that really makes sense.

Political statements are a mix of bluff and bluster, cliché and jargon, spiced up with an occasional gaffe about feeding the gondolas on the canal. The only time most politicians show any eloquence is when they get to insult each other, which is most of the time.

No wonder they spend much of their career doing impressions of demented lunatics and indulging in the sort of behaviour that would bring shame on a schoolyard bully. Even when they show some inspiration and come out with something visionary, people are likely to pick up what they want to hear rather than what the politician actually said.

Some of the most oft-quoted pieces of political rhetoric are infact misquotes. De Valera's comely maidens were not specifically dancing at the crossroads; Jack Lynch didn't talk of standing idly by; Oliver J. Flanagan didn't quite say there was no sex in Ireland before television; Brian Cowen never compared the Department of Health to Angola.

But, then again, the triumph of perception over oratory is not a peculiar Irish trait: Queen Victoria never complained that 'we are not amused' and Marie Antoinette never said anything about letting them eat cake. It all goes to show that where political rhetoric is concerned, beauty is in the ear of the begrudger.

Within these pages we have assembled a collection of the grand and the grandiose, the intentionally and unintentionally hilarious, the famous and infamous – decades of political leaders making fools of themselves for our entertainment. It is a reminder of why we vote for them in the first place.

EOGHAN CORRY
February 2007

Addresses to the Nation:

The Big Picture

The origin of the political speech was the address to the followers, to help them with their battles, to give them more money to pursue for their grandiose schemes, to trust them because they have a vision that the rest of us are too stupid to see. Alas, we keep falling for it.

'Acutely conscious though we all are of the misery and desolation in which the greater part of the world is plunged, let us turn aside for a moment to that ideal Ireland that we would have. That Ireland which we dreamed of would be the home of a people who valued material wealth only as the basis of right living, of a people who were satisfied with frugal comfort and devoted their leisure to the things of the spirit – a land whose countryside would be bright with cosy homesteads, whose fields and villages would be joyous with the sounds of industry, with the romping of sturdy children, the contests of athletic youths and the laughter of comely maidens, whose firesides would be forums for the wisdom of serene old age. It would, in a word, be the home of a people living the life that God desires that man should live.'

Eamon de Valera, radio broadcast, St Patrick's Day (1943).

'Ulster stands at the crossroads. There are, I know, today some so-called Loyalists who talk of independence from Britain – who seem to want a kind of Protestant Sinn Féin. Rhodesia, in defying Britain, at least has an air force and an army of her own. Where are the Ulster armoured divisions and the Ulster jet planes? Unionism armed with justice will be a stronger cause than Unionism armed merely with strength. What kind of Ulster do you want? A happy and respected province in good standing with the rest of the United Kingdom? Or a place continually torn apart by riots and demonstrations?'

Terence O'Neill, television address in response to civil rights demonstrations (9 December 1968).

'It is clear now that the present situation cannot be allowed to continue. It is evident that the Stormont Government is no longer in control of the situation. Indeed, the present situation is the inevitable outcome of the policies pursued for decades by successive Stormont Governments. It is clear also that the Irish Government can no longer stand by and see innocent people injured and perhaps worse.'

Jack Lynch, television address in response to Battle of the Bogside, when incursions by the Stormont regime police force into Catholic areas sparked off riots in Derry (13 August 1969). The words 'stand idly by', often attributed to Lynch, were included in an earlier, more moderate draft, which came before the cabinet from the Department of External Affairs.

Lynch's final version was "riddled with insertions and deletions all over the typed text".'
Stephen Collins, *The Power Game: Fianna Fáil since Lemass* (2000).

'I considered it my duty in the national interest to inform the Taoiseach of information I had received and which indicates a situation of such gravity for the nation that it is without parallel in this country since the foundation of the State . . . that those who were drawing public money to serve the nation were in fact attempting to undermine it.'
Liam Cosgrave, indicating he had knowledge of illegal importation of handguns by government ministers to supply to civil rights leaders (7 May 1970).

'It is obvious the RUC is no longer accepted as an impartial police force. Neither would the employment of British troops be acceptable nor would they be likely to restore peaceful conditions – certainly not in the long term. The Irish Government have therefore requested the British Government to apply immediately to the United Nations for the urgent despatch of a peace keeping force to the Six Counties. Recognising, however, that the reunification of the national territory can provide the only permanent solution for the problem, it is our intention to request the British Government to enter into early negotiations with the Irish Government to review the present constitutional position of the Six Counties of Northern Ireland. We have directed the Irish army authorities to have field hospitals established in County Donegal adjacent to Derry and other points along the border where they may be necessary.'
Jack Lynch, televison address in response to Battle of the Bogside (13 August 1969).

'I have but a few more words to say – I am going to my cold and silent grave – my lamp of life is nearly extinguished – my race is run – the grave opens to receive me, and I sink into its bosom. I have but one request to ask at my departure from this world; it is – the charity of its silence. Let no man write my epitaph; for as no man who knows my motives dare now vindicate them, let not prejudice or ignorance asperse them. Let them and me rest in obscurity and peace; and my tomb remain uninscribed, and my memory in oblivion, until other times and other men can do justice to my character.'

Robert Emmet, the speech from the dock, after he had been sentenced to death for leading a rising for Irish freedom from British rule (19 September 1803).

'Being convinced in our consciences that Home Rule would be disastrous to the material well-being of Ulster as well as of the whole of Ireland, subversive of our civil and religious freedom, destructive of our citizenship and perilous to the unity of the Empire, we, whose names are undersigned, men of Ulster, loyal subjects of His Gracious Majesty King George V, humbly relying on the God whom our fathers in days of stress and trial confidently trusted, do hereby pledge ourselves in solemn Covenant throughout this our time of threatened calamity to stand by one another in defending for ourselves and our children our cherished position of equal citizenship in the United Kingdom and in using all means which may be found necessary to defeat the present conspiracy to set up a Home Rule parliament in Ireland.'

Ulster's Solemn League and Covenant (28 September 1912).

'In the name of God and of the dead generations from which she received her old tradition of nationhood, Ireland, through us, summons her children to her flag and strikes for her freedom. We declare the right of the people of Ireland to the ownership of Ireland. Standing on that fundamental right and again asserting it in arms in the face of the world, we hereby proclaim the Irish Republic as a sovereign independent state.'

Proclamation, signed by Thomas J. Clarke, James Connolly, Sean MacDiarmada, Thomas MacDonagh, Padraig Pearse, Eamonn Ceannt, and Joseph Plunkett (24 April 1916).

'We place the cause of the Irish Republic under the protection of the Most High God, whose blessing we invoke upon our arms, and we pray that no one who serves that cause will dishonour it by cowardice, inhumanity, or rapine. In this supreme hour the Irish nation must, by its valour and discipline, and by the readiness of its children to sacrifice themselves for the common good, prove itself worthy of the august destiny to which it is called.'

Proclamation, signed by Thomas J. Clarke, James Connolly, Sean MacDiarmada, Thomas MacDonagh, Padraig Pearse, Eamonn Ceannt and Joseph Plunkett (24 April 1916).

'We, the elected representative of the ancient Irish people in National Parliament assembled, do, in the name of the Irish nation, ratify the establishment of the Irish Republic and pledge ourselves and our people to make this declaration effective by every means at our command.'

Dáil Éireann, Declaration of Independence, read at the first meeting in Dublin after winning 73 of 105 Irish seats in the General Election (21 January 1919).

'I, A.B., do solemnly swear (or affirm) that I do not and shall not yield a voluntary support to any pretended Government, authority or power within Ireland hostile and inimical thereto, and I do further swear (or affirm) that to the best of my knowledge and ability I will support and defend the Irish Republic and the Government of the Irish Republic, which is Dáil Éireann, against all enemies, foreign and domestic, and I will bear true faith and allegiance to the same, and that I take this obligation freely without any mental reservation or purpose of evasion, so help me, God.'

Oath to the Irish Republic, adopted by Dáil Éireann (20 August 1919).

'When my country takes her place among the nations of the earth, then, and not till then, let my epitaph be written.'

Robert Emmet, the speech from the dock, after he had been sentenced to death for leading a rising for Irish freedom from British rule (19 September 1803).

'It is war – and war in three days! Which letter am I to send? We must know your answer by 10 p.m. tonight. You can have until then but no longer to decide whether you will give peace or war to your country.'

David Lloyd-George, British Prime Minister, addressing Irish delegation at end of Treaty negotiations in London (5 December 1921).

'There are no overall certitudes in Ireland any more. There's a lot of diversity of thinking, a lot of uncertainty, a lot of trying to assimilate to other cultures. It's a time when we need to take stock, to look into our hearts and find a sense of Irishness, to find a pride in ourselves that will make us sure of what we are.'

Mary Robinson, during her presidential campaign (1990).

'You could say I came over to London to abstain in person.'

Frank Maguire, Independent Fermanagh-South Tyrone MP on refusing to vote to keep Labour in government (28 March 1979). Quoted in Conor O'Clery, *Ireland in Quotes: A History of the 20th Century* (1999).

'The oath to be taken by Members of the Parliament of the Irish Free State shall be in the following form: I . . . do solemnly swear the faith and allegiance to the Constitution of the Irish Free State as by law established and that I will be faithful to H.M. King George V, his heirs and successors by law, in virtue of the common citizenship of Ireland with Great Britain and her adherence to and membership of the group of nations forming the British Commonwealth of Nations.'

Paragraph 4, Articles of Agreement for a Treaty between Great Britain and Ireland (Anglo-Irish Treaty) signed by British and Irish delegations (6 December 1921).

'Any practical statesman will, under duress, swallow a dozen oaths to get his hand on the driving wheel.'

George Bernard Shaw, on Anglo-Irish Treaty, *Manchester Guardian* (27 December 1921).

'I solemnly swear that this oath is not an oath.'

Dan Breen, quoted in Breandán Ó hEithir, *The Begrudger's Guide to Irish Politics* (1986).

'I wish to talk to you this evening about the state of the nation's affairs, and the picture I have to paint is not, unfortunately, a very cheerful one. The figures which are just now becoming available to us show one thing very clearly.

As a community we are living away beyond our means . . . we have been living at a rate which is simply not justifiable by the amount of goods and services we are producing. To make up the difference we have been borrowing enormous amounts of money, borrowing at a rate which just cannot continue. A few simple figures will make this very clear . . . we will just have to reorganise government spending so that we can only undertake those things we can afford.'

Charles J. Haughey, speech to the Irish nation as Taoiseach (9 January 1980).

'Only the government can achieve a balance between national resources and the often conflicting desires of every section and take the decisions which determine the rate of economic or social progress and keep the country moving in line on a common front. As president Kennedy said 'A rising tide lifts all the boats'.'

Sean Lemass, Dáil Éireann (15 April 1964)

'I very nearly, if not actually, declared the Republic – in Ottawa of all places. I will explain when I return why I decided to state publicly that we intended to repeal the External Relations Act. It was really the article in the *Sunday Independent* that decided me.'

John A. Costello, on his decision to declare Ireland a Republic (11 September 1948).

'The two governments . . . affirm that any change in the status of Northern Ireland would only come about with the consent of a majority of the people of Northern Ireland.'

Article 1, Anglo-Irish Agreement, Hillsborough Castle, County Down (1985).

Agriculture

It is not clear where the Irish obsession with agriculture came from, but it dominated the economics of pre-independence Ireland and the political philosophy of the first generation of politicians after independence. Agricultural prices determined the course of logical politics, and the occasional revolution. The boom of the 1780s and collapse in prices in 1796 were among the sparks of the 1798 rebellion. Wheat prices determined matters in large parts of the country in the nineteenth century, and when independence arrived, both the main parties in the Free State and the main party in the north all stressed agriculture as the great way forward. Miraculously, despite all the meddling, we still have a thriving agri-food industry.

'For forty-six years the people of Ireland have been feeding those of England with the choicest produce of their agriculture and pasture; and while they thus exported their wheat and their beef in profusion, their own food became gradually deteriorated in each successive year, until the mass of the peasantry was exclusively thrown on the potato.'

John MacHale, Archbishop of Tuam, letter to British Prime Minister John Russell, after he blocked proposals to alleviate the famine in Ireland (15 December 1846).

'One more cow, one more sow, and one more acre under the plough.'

Patrick Hogan, Minister for Agriculture, slogan to promote farming growth (1 February 1922). Quoted in J.J. Lee, *Ireland 1912-1985: Politics and Society* (1989).

'If the British Government should succeed in beating us in this fight, then you could have no freedom, because at every step they could threaten you again and force you again to obey the British. What is involved is whether the Irish nation is going to be free or not.'

Eamon de Valera, on economic war with Britain over Ireland's refusal to pay land annuities to London (November 1932). Quoted in Ronan Fanning, *Independent Ireland* (1983).

'I suggest there have been more idiotic theories in connection with agriculture than with any other industry in the country. These idiotic theories are particularly rife amongst non-farmers. Teachers, doctors, politicians and lawyers of all sorts all have their theories about agriculture.'

Patrick Hogan, Minister for Agriculture, Dáil Éireann (3 November 1932).

'What is a fair day now? It is a standing nightmare to every person in the country. What was in the past a monthly occasion upon which they got a bit of fun out of life has now become a monthly horror in which people drive cattle into the fair, stand in the usual unpleasant circumstances on a fair green on a wet day, are never asked where they were going, or else bid a price which they know is less than it cost to produce the cattle.'

James Dillon, TD for West Donegal, Dáil Éireann (3 November 1932). James Dillon went on to become deputy leader of Fine Gael under William T. Cosgrave.

'The portrayal of the department man as a person accustomed to transacting business in public houses and having dubious financial dealings with farmers to whom he is rendering a service on behalf of the government is considered by our members to be nothing short of libellous.'

R.B. Pares, General Secretary of Institute of Professional Civil Servants, complaining to RTÉ over the portrayal of an agricultural adviser on the Radio 1 show The Riordans (1969).

'We have reached the point where a collapse of our economic system is in sight. By a collapse I mean famine conditions for a large number of our people.'

Seán Lemass, Minister for Industry and Commerce, memo to Eamon de Valera, President of the Executive Council, on the economic war with Britain (1 November 1932). Quoted in Ronan Fanning, Independent Ireland (1983).

'The State is lying, panting, exhausted by her own weight, and being rent by a farrow of cannibal piglets.'

John Kelly, Fine Gael TD, The Irish Times (22 August 1981).

'A farmer has four or five sons. He cannot keep them all on the land and he sends some of them to the university to be made doctors or solicitors or barristers. He keeps Jack at home. He has got to earn his livelihood, and he has to work hard and keep Tom in college with polished boots, shirts, collars and ties. After a certain number of years in college, Tom is turned out as a barrister, briefless or otherwise, and Jack, working on the land, has to keep him for another time, and to keep the others in or out of college.'

Dan Corry, Fianna Fail TD for North Cork, Dáil Éireann. Corry's jousts with Fine Gael's James Dillon entertained the Dáil gallery for three decades (4 May 1934).

'Clann na Talmhan was unique among Irish political parties to gain representation in Dáil Éireann by having almost no policies apart from remedying farmers' grievances: a task beyond human, or even divine, competence.'

Breandán Ó hEithir, *The Begrudger's Guide to Irish Politics* (1986).

'National development in Ireland, for our generation at least, is practically synonymous with agricultural development.'

Patrick Hogan, Minister for Agriculture (25 January 1924). Quoted in J.J. Lee, *Ireland 1912–1985: Politics and Society* (1989).

'I am going to smother Britain in eggs.'

James Dillon, after he was appointed Minister for Agriculture (1948). In rural areas small chicks were nicknamed 'Dillons' in reference to his poultry-expansionist policies.

Bertie Ahern

The rise of Bartholomew Ahern to become the Taoiseach during the period of greatest prosperity in Irish history is all the more remarkable when you realise how small a part speechifying has in his life. Bertie's speeches are sound bites, often uncomplimentary to himself. With the eleventh Taoiseach, less is more. And who minds if the 'THs' are hardened or turned into 'Ds'? The ultimate TD.

'He's the cleverest, the most cunning, the best of the lot.'
Charles J. Haughey, on Bertie Ahern (16 October 1991).
Sometimes quoted as 'the most skilful, most cunning, most devious of them all'.

'When I will be Taoiseach.'
Bertie Ahern, school essay, aged thirteen.

'I have probably more deep political views than most people.'
Bertie Ahern (1994).

'In political life you have a hassle period of some difficulties. I'm neither separated nor the best family man in the world. I'm somewhere in between.'

Bertie Ahern, on his private life, *The Irish Times* (6 April 1991).

'Ah Bertie, great little gurrier. Bertie, salt of the earth. Reminds me of myself before I made my first million. Smashing kid. One day, Mara, one day, mark my words, young Bertie will sit where I now sit. I am going to see he is my successor.'

Sketch on satirical radio programme *Scrap Saturday*, scripted by Owen Roe, Gerry Stembridge and Dermot Morgan (1991).

'It would be an absolute fairytale coming from background of no wealth or power in the family. If Bertie goes for the leadership of Fianna Fáil he will win. The figures will be right.'

Noel Ahern, member of Dáil Éireann, talking to the *Irish Press* about whether Bertie Ahern could become Taoiseach (1992).

'He is undoubtedly the most gifted political operator of his or any other generation.'

Frank Dunlop, on Bertie Ahern, in *Yes Taoiseach: Irish Politics from Behind Closed Doors* (2004).

'I will not oppose you.'

Bertie Ahern, commitment to Albert Reynolds, before voting for Charles J. Haughey as new leader of the Fianna Fáil party (1992).

'I went to extraordinary lengths to investigate the matter.

I was up every tree in North Dublin. I know the circumstances about it and I am quite satisfied with the matter.'

Bertie Ahern, interview with Gerald Barry on the RTÉ radio programme *This Week*, referring to his investigations into corruption allegations against the Minister for Foreign Affairs, Ray Burke (23 May 1997).

Anybody who knows my relationship with Mr Haughey would have been just either not telling the truth or a lunatic to believe that.'

Bertie Ahern, explaining decision to vote for Charles J. Haughey as leader of Fianna Fáil party against Albert Reynolds (November 1992).

'All I wanted was to do me budget.'

Bertie Ahern, on changing his stance during the Fianna Fáil leadership heave (1992). Quoted in Katie Hannon, *The Naked Politician* (2004).

'We owe it to the least fortunate of our citizens to ensure that public decisions affecting everyone's welfare are taken only on grounds of and for the public good, and to ensure that possession of wealth can never privately purchase political favours.'

Bertie Ahern, the speech that effectively distanced himself from allegations of corruption which ruined the reputations of former colleagues Charles Haughey and Ray Burke (25 August 1997).

Bertie Ahern (on being asked the price of a loaf of bread and a litre of milk): 'Probably a lot more knowledgeable but I do not think that people find it all gobbledegook because the fact is you cannot run the health services, the educational services and the other services in the country if you have not got your overall framework right and that's the same with a person in their household. A person in a household has to take into account what take-home pay they have every week, what goes to their mortgage, what goes to their milk and their sliced pan. They are the important issues for people I do [know] and I certainly would have. After the last six months or so because I think I've been in every shopping park in the country.'

Reporter: 'How much is it?'

Bertie Ahern: 'I know . . . I know how much they are. I'm not going to start playing games with you but I do know. I'm still not bad at shopping.'

Reporter: 'How much?'

Bertie Ahern: 'In actual fact – back where . . . I think you were beside me back in O'Neill's in Drumcondra when you were following me, I go in and do my own shopping nearly every day so I'm fairly . . .'

Bertie Ahern, to TV3 reporter during election campaign (2002).

'My philosophy is Republicanism. I am left of centre; I think everybody knows I'm left of centre.'

Bertie Ahern, on his political philosophy (2002).

'I was not in the House yesterday when the Labour Party leader asked the Taoiseach about his new-found commitment to socialism. Ironically, I was abroad for several days on political work to advance the cause of socialism. You can imagine, a Ceann Comhairle, how perplexed I was when

I returned to find my wardrobe almost empty. The Taoiseach had been busy robbing my clothes. Up to recently, the Progressive Democrats did not have a stitch left due to the same Taoiseach but we never expected him to take a walk on the left side of the street. He said: "I am one of the few socialists left in Irish politics." Immediately, Tomás Ó Criomhthaín came to mind, as he lamented the last of the Blasket Islanders: Ní bheidh ár leithéidí arís ann. I then thought: Good, Taoiseach. There are two of us in it and we will go down together.'

Joe Higgins, Socialist TD (17 November 2005).

'I am one of the few socialists left in Irish politics.'

Bertie Ahern, interview with Mark Brennock, *The Irish Times* (13 November 2004).

'There are only four socialists in the Dáil and Bertie is one of them.'

Charlie McCreevy, European Commissioner for Internal Market and Services (July 2005).

'I have no big houses or mansions or yachts or studs. All I've got is a mortgage. The only thing that they have on me is the fact that my marriage has broken down and I'm with Celia. I know all the rumours and so do Celia and Miriam. I can do sweet nothing about these things. You can sound me out till the cows come home: you'll find no Garda reports, no barring orders, nothing. I'll tell you there's not a whole many things that I can swear 110 per cent on, because I am no more an angel than anyone else in this life, but of the barring orders there is zilch.'

Bertie Ahern, quoted in Ken Whelan and Eugene Masterson, *Bertie Ahern: Taoiseach and Peacemaker* (1998).

'I am not answering what I got on my Holy Communion money, my Confirmation money, what I got for my birthday, what I got for anything else. I'm not into that.'

Bertie Ahern, Dáil Éireann, answering allegations of private payments he received (21 September 2006).

'The only way we will ever succeed in helping the people in need is having a strong economy that generates the wealth so that we can redistribute the wealth.'

Bertie Ahern, interview with Mark Brennock, *The Irish Times* (13 November 2004)

'Ah jaysus, lads, you'll have me in huge trouble if you don't take back the £50,000. My circumstances have improved, and I will have 50 reporters traipsing me for the rest of my life if this comes out. Bertie.'

Joe Higgins, Socialist TD, parodies Bertie Ahern in Dáil Éireann (27 September 2006).

'Tell Paddy the plasterer to stay clear of Calelly's house. He is in enough trouble with the painter already.'

Joe Higgins, Socialist TD, parodies Bertie Ahern in Dáil Éireann (27 September 2006).

Noel Browne

Striding over the political history of the capital city, and to some extent the island, is a doctor who was Minister for Health for a brief three-year period. His name has come to personify the battle between the modern caring state and its paternalistic predecessor. He created some of his own mythology with embittered interviews and the biggest-selling political memoir in Irish history, but the myth is not entirely his own creation. His spat was not with the Catholic Church, initially at least, but with his medical colleagues who saw free health as a threat to their lucrative incomes, earned on the back of TB, the disease he eradicated. His biggest quarrel was not with the Taoiseach, but with his party leader. The Government didn't fall because of the Mother and Child Scheme, it broke up in a spat over agricultural prices. The Free Health Scheme he tried to introduce was brought in by Fianna Fáil two years later with scarcely a whimper from either medics or bishops. But in politics, perception is everything, and Browne is one of the most fascinating people to emerge from outside the traditional strands of Irish political history.

'[It is] unworthy of members of the medical profession to try
to confuse the simple matter of pounds, shillings and pence
with questions of high principles and morality.'

Noel Browne (11 July 1950).

'I reflected that one Judas was bad enough, but twelve of
them must be some kind of record, even in Ireland.'

Noel Browne, on his government colleagues, two days after
the Mother and Child Scheme had been condemned by the
Roman Catholic Hierarchy on the urgings of the Irish
Medical Organisation, and four days before Tánaiste and his
party leader Seán MacBride requested his resignation (6 April
1951).

'The Bishop of Galway took up a question dear to his heart,
that of the burden of rates and taxation. He claimed that it
was unfair to tax the rest of the community in order to give
the poor a free health service.'

Noel Browne, *Against The Tide* (1986).

'While, as I have said, I as a Catholic accept unequivocally
and unreservedly the views of the Hierarchy on this matter,
I have not been able to accept the manner in which this
matter has been dealt with by my former colleagues in the
Government.'

Noel Browne, the day after resigning as Minister for Health
on Seán MacBride's request (12 April 1951).

'For the last year, in my view, the Minister for Health has not
been normal.'

Seán MacBride, Tánaiste, Clann na Poblachta leader and
Minister of Foreign Affairs (12 April 1951).

'It's a one-party state. There's no significant difference between any of the parties at the present time.
Fianna Fáil, Fine Gael, Labour, they're all utterly inter-
changeable.'

Noel Browne, quoted in *The Irish Times* (20 November
1996).

'We took power down here in the Republic from Britain and
handed it over then, effectively, to the other great imperial
power, Rome.'

Noel Browne, quoted in *The Irish Times* (20 November
1996).

'Clann na Poblachta was born in high drama, lived on the edge
for much of its early political existence and came to grief in
unbelievably theatrical circumstances.'

Eithne MacDermott, Clann na Poblachta (1998).

'When they failed so miserably on the first fence of giving
mothers and children a better health service, you have to
wonder whether they were serious.'

Noel Browne, on Clann na Poblachta, quoted in *The Irish
Times* (20 November 1996).

'When will the profession of politics in the Republic, on the
success of which depends the happiness of all of us, become
the supreme vocation, whose practice demands not just fair
weather, self-indulgent tinkering, but a lifelong dedication,
unlimited political scholarship, and literacy at the highest
level?'

Noel Browne, quoted in *The Irish Times* (10 June 1997).

'He was a loner, of course, committed more to the struggle than to the political life. His allegiance was to the mass of people who struggled, rather than to any organisation.'

Dick Spring, tribute to Noel Browne (23 May 1997).

'The beautiful children who could have been musicians, artists, writers and scientists and all the marvellous things that education can bring to any one of us. They were denied all of these because the average family simply couldn't afford the fees needed to educate so many boys and girls. They ended up as coolie labour in countries all over the world.'

Noel Browne, quoted in *The Irish Times* (20 November 1996).

'Dr Browne began by "abject apology" for troubling me on such a day. Described his notes and impressions concerning our interview in October. I told him exactly how he had behaved. He was very surprised and apologised, saying he had been very nervous. Browne asked me to believe he wanted to be only a good Catholic and to accept fully the Church's teaching. Dr Browne then said: "Well, that is the end. It will be very serious for the government and the people and me. I shall leave the cabinet and political life. It is a rotten life".'

Notes in John Charles McQuaid's diary (Holy Thursday 1951).

'In defeat, Noel Browne had one glorious round which won him his permanent place in the record books. For the first time in the history of the state, anyone who could read and who had the price of a newspaper got the inside story of

what happened when the Church set out to bend politicians
to its will. It was all there because Browne had made the
necessary arrangements with the editor of *The Irish Times*
and that ensured that all the other papers carried the
correspondence also.'

Breandán Ó hEithir, *The Begrudger's Guide to Irish Politics*
(1986).

John Bruton

The tenth Taoiseach was honed on the high rhetoric of farmers' protests during the 1960s but never quite got the hang of it himself. He didn't perform well either on the podium or for the television cameras; his laugh was the subject of satire; but it didn't seem to matter. He became Taoiseach in mid-term, expressing shock at his appointment, and left two years later having pulled together a disparate and eccentric bunch of characters and moulded them into a coherent government. He wasn't as shocked as some of his own followers that it all came together so well.

'It's stimulating to talk to him because he is a ferment of new ideas, but if you are not in the business of wanting a ferment, then it can be a bit confusing.'
Alan Dukes, on John Bruton, *The Irish Times* (January 1993).

'I'm sick of answering questions about the fucking peace process. I am the Taoiseach. My job is to run the country.'
John Bruton, interview with Cathy Farrell of Cork Radio 96FM (1995).

'The Government must go about its work without excess or extravagance and as transparently as if it were working behind a pane of glass.'

John Bruton, speech on his election as Taoiseach (15 December 1994).

'Is Charlie Bird in the bushes? Good. That means I won't be asked about the fucking peace process.'

John Bruton, on a visit to Indigo, making light of the furore that erupted over his Cork Radio 96FM interview (December 1995).

'John gives a hostage to fortune right away, saying the government must always be seen operating behind a pane of glass. That'll be the day.'

Seán Duignan, *One Spin on the Merry-Go-Round* (1995).

'If the Air Corps has a frequent-flyer programme, government ministers could probably get to the moon and back on their accumulated points.'

John Bruton (14 October 1994).

Budget Day

The one day of the year when politicians do what they are supposed to do, as in deciding how much tax they collect and how they spend it. Both questions have perplexed them endlessly through political history. The more bankrupt the economy, the more exciting the budget. Theatrical gestures were born, with finance ministers posing outside the Dáil with bulging briefcases (and in one case, a thoroughly modern computer CD-ROM) followed by fractious reactions from opposition spokespeople who hadn't got time to digest what had just been proposed. The average length of a speech went from over two hours (in the time of Ernest Blythe, Seán MacEntee and even longer in the case of Richie Ryan) to forty-one minutes (by 'galloping' Charlie McCreevy). Legends are created about a shilling being taken off the old-age pension, tax being put on children's shoes and stallions being allowed to have sex for free. One minister was photographed with his briefcase by an evening newspaper despite the fact that he had fallen off a horse and never made it to the Dáil to present the budget in the first place. The lesson for us all is to watch the fine print: the budget of 1952 sent the entire economy into a ten-year recession because nobody noticed what was going on inside that battered briefcase.

'To tax and to please, no more than to love and be wise, is not given to men.'
Edmund Burke, speech on American taxation (1774).

'It is, I think, also undeniable that the reduction of a shilling in the maximum pension does not leave the pensioner any worse off than that pensioner was a couple of years ago, when the value of money was less than it is at the present time.'
Ernest Blythe (3 April 1924).

'I have a great deal of respect for the Taoiseach in a great many matters. I think he has rendered considerable service to this country, but when it comes to economics I think he knows nothing about them.'
Seán MacBride, to Taoiseach Eamon de Valera in Dáil Éireann (2 April 1952).

'I say that the Budget speech of the Minister is a clear and definite proclamation to boys and girls in the rural areas to fly out of the country while the going is good.'
Joe Blowick TD, response to the budget (2 April 1952).

'The fevered spending of the Marshall period is over. It is now a matter of urgent importance to arrange that where our expenditure is current expenditure, it will be financed from taxation or other normal sources of revenue, and that in so far as it is of a genuine capital nature, we shall endeavour to meet it out of the current savings of the Irish public.'

Seán MacEntee, Minister for Finance, speech introducing the deflationary budget that sent the Irish economy into freefall (23 April 1952). Quoted in Diarmaid Ferriter, *What If? Alternative Views of Twentieth Century Ireland* (2006).

'Before leaving his home this morning the Minister for Finance met with an accident which has resulted in concussion. He is now in hospital and has been ordered to remain under medical observation for a few days.'

Jack Lynch, Taoiseach, address to Dáil about Charles J. Haughey on Budget Day (22 April 1970). Rumours had spread about the nature of the injury.

'The fruits of fifteen years' labour are beginning to be frittered away.'

T.K. Whitaker, ex-Finance Secretary, in response to the budget of 1972. Paraphrased in *J.J. Lee, Ireland 1912–1985: Politics and Society* (1989).

'The economy is, for the third year in succession, running at well below capacity. Unemployment is high. We lack the economic buoyancy required to tackle quickly and effectively the adaptation which membership of the EEC will demand.'

George Colley, Minister for Finance (19 April 1972).

'That Budget story is an enduring myth of Irish politics. I am afraid that my own post-Budget actions were to blame for the emergence of this myth. I was moved to reveal the Department of Finance had argued that because some women had smaller feet than some children such a

distinction should not be made. This argument had tickled my fancy during the pre-Budget cabinet discussions, and had stuck in my mind.'
Garret FitzGerald (9 September 2000).

'The Budget was defeated because, while Noel Browne supported it, Jim Kemmy and Mr Loftus voted against. If the issue that concerned Jim Kemmy was the modification of the food subsidies, where did the legend about the Budget falling on the issue of children's shoes originate?'
Garret FitzGerald (9 September 2000).

'They took me for granted. That was the mistake they made last night. It might seem pompous for me to say it, but I feel I was entitled to influence the Government more than I did.'
Jim Kemmy TD (27 January 1982).

'The underestimation of current deficits, and consequently of the Exchequer Borrowing Requirement, has been so seriously disproportionate as to invalidate the whole budgetary exercise.'
T.K. Whitaker (1983).

'This is grand larceny of our policy as put before the electorate.'
Michael Noonan TD, speech on the budget of 1987, quoted in Bruce Arnold, *Haughey, his Life and Unlucky Deeds* (1993).

'The Irish Economy – Celtic Tiger or Tortoise.'
Kevin Gardner, economist, Morgan Stanley report (31 August 1994). First reference to 'Celtic Tiger' in an official document was in study by Dr Antóin Murphy, mentioned in Dáil Éireann (16 February 1995). The term was later popularised by the media work of another economist, David McWilliams.

'You either spend on public expenditure or tax reductions. As Minister for Finance and as a person who believes taxes are too high in this country, I personally would rather see that going on tax reductions. But that is not what I am hearing from just about every group in the country.'

Bertie Ahern, Minister for Finance, introducing budget which was to lift the Irish economy (1992).

'This is where we sit and listen to McCreevy.'

John O'Donoghue TD, Minister for Arts, Sport and Tourism, on the television programme *Hanging with Hector* (2004).

'You will get a rare opportunity to gain access to the Minister in a semi-formal environment.'

Eithne Fitzgerald TD, Minister of the Department of Enterprise and Employment, in a letter inviting party supporters to attend a £100-a-plate dinner with Finance Minister Ruairi Quinn (27 February 1996).

'Nobody would attempt to leak a confidential document by faxing it to the press with their name attached.'

Phil Hogan TD, resigns as Minister for State over a budget leak (9 February 1995).

Buzzwords

Who invented them? When did they stop being funny and become a cliché? The history of the well-worn phrase in Irish history is going to be an inexact and folkloric exercise, but a few phrases are worthy of mention.

1970   Arms Crisis

1971   Deep interrogation

1972   Irish dimension

1973   Power-sharing

1974   Contraception

1976   Thundering disgrace

1977   Heavy gang

1978   Ulsterisation

1979   Irish solution for an Irish problem

1980   Ireland Inc.

1981	Privatisation
1982	GUBU
1983	Democratic deficit
1984	Supply-side economics
1985	Recessionary times
1986	Ulster says no
1987	Tallaght Strategy
1988	Economic fundamentals
1989	Sustainable growth
1990	Mature recollection
1991	Liberal agenda
1992	Pan-Nationalist Front
1993	Third sector of the economy
1994	Parity of esteem
1995	Window of opportunity
1996	The extra mile
1997	Demilitarisation/decommissioning
1998	Celtic Tiger
1999	Dead-man defence
1999	Brown envelopes
2000	Forward-looking
2001	9/11
2002	Benchmarking

2003 Decentralisation
2004 Lower growth trajectories
2005 Capital envelopes
2006 Going forward

Churchmen
and Croziers at Dawn

Politicians don't like to be hindered in the pursuit of power. While the electorate, the media, the unions and the farmers occasionally try their best to keep them in check, their efforts in out-playing the politicians at politics pale into insignificance compared with the main Christian churches. Until the 1980s, the churches held a trump card. When no one was looking, 100 years earlier, they had taken control of the education and health systems (and, bizarrely, the orphanages and juvenile prisons). It meant they could drive debates on censorship, divorce and abortion without appearing to participate. When the tide finally turned and the Catholic Church had to take its place in the queue of pressure groups beside unmarried mothers and heroin addicts, the politicians had a field day, blaming the Church for everything that went wrong over the previous six decades – including the problems caused by the politicians themselves.

'I'm not a fascist. I'm a priest. Fascists dress up in black and tell people what to do. Whereas priests . . .'

Fr Ted Crilly (Dermot Morgan), in the television series *Father Ted*, scripted by Arthur Mathews and Graham Linehan (1995–8).

'Trí cuil túaithe: flaith brécach, breithem gúach, sacart colach.' ('Three ruins of a tribe: a lying chief, a false judge, a lustful priest.')

Kuno Meyer, *The Triads of Ireland* (14th century).

'St Patrick brought Christianity to Ireland. It is a pity the idea never caught on.'

George Bernard Shaw (attrib.).

'As to what is called Fenianism, you are aware that looking on it as a compound of folly and wickedness wearing a mask of patriotism, and as the work of a few fanatics and knaves, wicked enough to jeopardise others in order to promote their own sordid views.'

Cardinal Paul Cullen, pastoral letter (10 October 1865).

'When we look down into the fathomless depths of the Fenian conspiracy, we must acknowledge that eternity is not long enough nor hell hot enough for such miscreants.'

Bishop David Moriarty, sermon given in Kerry (February 1867).

'It is intended to affect the domain of morals alone, and in no way to interfere with politics as such in the country.'

Catholic hierarchy, statement in response to the papal rescript issued by the Vatican two months earlier condemning the Plan of Campaign and boycotting, a result of the London government's Persico Mission to get Vatican support for their policies in Ireland (2 June 1888).

'Methods of warfare known as boycotting and the Plan of Campaign may not lawfully be used.'
Pope Leo XIII, taking issue with the Irish Hierarchy (24 June 1888).

'The time has long since gone when Irish men and Irish women could be kept from thinking by hurling priestly thunder at their heads.'
James Connolly, *Labour, Nationality and Religion* (1910).

'The fight for Irish freedom has passed into the hands of the young men of Ireland [. . .] and when the young men of Ireland hit back at their oppressors it is not for an old man like me to cry "foul".'
Michael Fogarty, Bishop of Killaloe (23 January 1919).

'It is one of the glories of the Church in which I was born that we have put our bishops in their places in discussions requiring legislation. Even in those discussions involving legislation on matters of religion they count only according to their individual intelligence and knowledge. The rights of divorce, and many other rights, were won by the Protestant communities in the teeth of the most-bitter opposition from their clergy.'
W.B. Yeats, challenging the Church of Ireland Bishop of Meath Benjamin John Plunket for supporting divorce legislation in Seanad Éireann (11 June 1925).

'If your girls don't obey you, if they are not back in at the hours appointed, lay the lash upon their backs.'

Thomas O'Doherty, Bishop of Galway, quoted in Breandán Ó hEithir, *The Begrudger's Guide to Irish Politics* (1986).

'The State is not entitled to relieve the 10 per cent of necessitous or negligent parents by infringing the rights of the other 90 per cent of parents to provide for the health of their children.'

Catholic hierarchy, statement on Mother and Child scheme (1948).

'Their public roads adjacent to cities and towns are a scandal and a shame to decent citizens and to the young and innocent a positive danger in the most brazen and audacious manner. The love scenes of the cinema are reproduced in the public roadsides to the scandal and offence of all. A very great evil, not dead yet, was the dancehall without supervision or control, often with excessive drinking and unashamed company keeping and late hours, with the saddest results to virtue and morality, as had been seen in the public courts for the last few years.'

Patrick Collier, Bishop of Ossory, Lenten Pastoral (1928).

'If I had a vote on a local body, and if there were two qualified people who had to deal with a Catholic community, and if one was a Catholic and the other a Protestant, I would unhesitatingly vote for the Catholic.'

Eamon de Valera (17 June 1931).

'If you show that this country, Southern Ireland, is going to be governed by Catholic ideas and by Catholic ideas alone you will put a wedge into the midst of this nation. We, against whom you have done this thing, are no petty people.

We are one of the great stocks of Europe. We are the people of Burke; we are the people of Grattan; we are the people of Swift, the people of Emmet, the people of Parnell. We have created most of the modern literature of this country. We have created the best of its political intelligence.'

W.B. Yeats, debate on divorce, Seanad Éireann (11 June 1925).

'Our zealot's idea of establishing the Kingdom of God upon earth is to make Ireland an island of moral cowards.'

W.B. Yeats, *Manchester Guardian*, protesting against proposal to establish censorship board (22 September 1928).

'During the intervals [between dances] the devil is busy; yes very busy, as sad experience proves, and on the way home in the small hours of the morning he is busier still.'

Catholic hierarchy (20 December 1933).

'Since the coming of St Patrick, fifteen hundred years ago, Ireland has been a Christian and a Catholic nation. All the ruthless attempts made through the centuries to force her from this allegiance have not shaken her faith. She remains a Catholic nation.'

Eamon de Valera, radio broadcast to the USA (17 March 1935).

'Our young are leaving Ireland to take up employment in circumstances, and under conditions, which, in many cases, are full of danger to their religious and moral well-being.'

Catholic hierarchy (7 October 1947).

'On the occasion of our assumption of office and our first cabinet meeting, my colleagues and myself desire to repose at the feet of Your Holiness the assurance of our filial joy and of our devotion, as well as our firm resolve to be guided in all our work by the teaching of Christ and to strive for the attainment of a social order in Ireland based on Christian principles.'

John A. Costello (23 February 1948). Quoted in David McCullagh, *Makeshift Majority* (1998).

'Ireland is the only place I could go – only there would I have the atmosphere and the sense of security to rule the Church as Christ want me to rule it.'

Pope Pius XII, replying to Irish offer of refuge if communists took over Italy (25 February 1948). Quoted in Dermot Keogh, *Twentieth-Century Ireland* (1994).

'We shall have saved the country from advancing a long way towards socialistic welfare.'

Archbishop John Charles McQuaid, on the Mother and Child Scheme (1948) quoted in Maev-Ann Wren, *Unhealthy State: Anatomy of a Sick Society* (2003).

'The powers taken by the State in the proposed Mother and Child Health Service are in direct opposition to the rights of the family and of the individual and are liable to very great abuse . . . If adopted in law, they would constitute a ready-made instrument for future totalitarian aggression.'

An Irish bishop, letter to Taoiseach John A. Costello (10 October 1950).

'How can any Catholic logically demand or permit any legislation which would endanger the soul of a single child? Take the case of a Catholic girl who . . . hands her child over to kindly people not of her faith. When that mother has rehabilitated herself and become more normal, she will know that she has done wrong.'

Charles Casey, Attorney General, defending refusal of the government to introduce legal adoptions (13 February 1951).

'Whatever about fighting the doctors, I will not fight the bishops, and whatever about fighting the bishops, I will not fight the doctors and the bishops together.'

John A. Costello, Taoiseach (14 March 1951).

'Our decision expresses the complete willingness of the Government to defer to the judgement so given by the Hierarchy.'

John A. Costello, Taoiseach (9 April 1951).

'The most serious revelation, however, is that the Roman Catholic Church would seem to be the effective government of this country.'

The Irish Times (12 April 1951).

'The creation of a situation where it is made to appear that a conflict exists between the spiritual and temporal authorities is always undesirable; in the case of Ireland, it is highly damaging to the cause of national unity.'

Seán MacBride, Tánaiste, Clann na Poblachta leader and Minister of Foreign Affairs (10 April 1951).

'The Hierarchy cannot approve of any scheme which, in its general tendency, must foster undue control by the State in a sphere so delicate and so intimately concerned with morals as

that which deals with gynaecology or obstetrics and with the relations between doctor and patient.'
Catholic Bishops (5 April 1951).

'The power and the spirit behind practically all social legislation at the present time take the worst principles of both Nazi and Russian materialism.'
Dr Neil Farren, Bishop of Derry (17 April 1951).

'The establishment of this [Mother and Child] scheme would soon eliminate the free medical practitioner and create a monopoly of socialised medical services under complete state control – a terrible weapon to put into the hands of men who might not have received instruction in Catholic principles, or who might repudiate such principles.'
Dr Michael Browne, Bishop of Galway (30 April 1951).

'The Dáil proposes; Maynooth disposes.'
Seán Ó Faoláin, writer (1 June 1951).

'Free hospital services would seriously weaken the moral fibre of the people.'
Catholic hierarchy, opposing the Health Act that extended responsibility of county councils on health on the grounds that it was undue State interference in family affairs (1953).

'I regard this boycott as ill-conceived, ill-considered and futile for the achievement of the purpose for which it seems to have been intended; [and] I regard it as unjust and cruel to confound the innocent with the guilty.'
Eamon de Valera, condemning the boycott of Protestant businesses in Fethard-on-Sea (4 July 1957).

'The bishops fully share the disquiet . . . regarding pressures being exerted on public opinion on questions concerning the civil law on divorce, contraception and abortion . . . Civil law on these matters should respect the wishes of the people who elected the legislators and the bishops confidently hope that the legislators themselves will respect this important principle.'

Catholic hierarchy (11 March 1971).

'I don't want to get a belt of the crozier.'

Sean MacEoin (13 February 1951).

'When the bishops in this country took a stand not so long ago on the Health Bill . . . their position was that they were the final arbiters of right and wrong, even in political matters.'

Dr Lucey, Bishop of Cork and Ross (12 April 1955).

'You may have been worried by much talk of changes to come. Allow me to reassure you. No change will worry the tranquility of your Christian lives.'

John Charles McQuaid, Archbishop of Dublin (10 December 1965).

'Legislators in a plural society should guard against considering matters solely from the standpoint of their personal religious practices.'

Patrick Hillery, Minister for External Affairs (9 March 1971).

'Any such contraceptive act is always wrong in itself. [Legalising contraceptives] would be an insult to our faith, a curse upon our country.'

John Charles McQuaid, Archbishop of Dublin (March 1971).

'Among the best traitors Ireland has ever had, Mother Church ranks at the very top, a massive obstacle in the path to equality and freedom.'

Bernadette Devlin, *The Price of My Soul* (1969).

'Let us hope and trust that there are sufficient proud and ignorant people left in this country to stand up to the intellectuals who are out to destroy faith and fatherland.'

Oliver J. Flanagan TD (10 April 1971).

'Men still speak today of completing the unfinished business of 1916–1922. There is, after fifty years, much unfinished business still to do for Ireland. But the weapons of its completion are no longer rifles and grenades. The tools of Irish patriotism now are not the drill of war but the politics and economics of social justice and the structures of inter-community peace.'

Dr Cathal Daly, Bishop of Ardagh and Clonmacnoise, during funeral of Lieutenant-General Sean MacEoin, member of old IRA and former Justice Minister (10 July 1973).

'I have met more clergy of all denominations in the past eighteen months than in the whole of my previous life. Time will tell if it has done me any good.'

William Whitelaw, Secretary of State for Northern Ireland (13 October 1973).

'No change in state law can make the use of contraceptives morally right . . . It does not follow of course that the State is bound to prohibit the importation and sale of contraceptives.'

Catholic hierarchy (25 November 1973).

'Contraceptives will affect marital fidelity and mean a general extension of promiscuity . . . There is a contagion in these things. The effect seems to spread.'

Cardinal William Conway (2 December 1973).

'We have never asked as a Church that our moral law be reflected in the civil law.'

Dr Eamon Casey, Bishop of Kerry (23 May 1975).

'Pandering to the whim of those who wish to keep Ballymena's swimming pool open on Sundays would open the gates for a flood of godlessness such as Ulster has never seen.'

John McAuley, DUP Mayor of Ballymena (4 January 1978).

'Patrick you chatter too loud / And lift your crozier too high / Your stick would be kindling soon / If my son Osgar stood by.'

Frank O'Connor, translation of an earlier record of a spat between Church and state from the fifth century.

'Love is never defeated, and I could add, the history of Ireland proves it.'

Pope John Paul II, address in Galway (30 September 1979).

'Pervading Nationalism imposes its dominion on man today in many different forms and with an aggressiveness that spares no one [. . .] The challenge that is already with us is the temptation to accept as true freedom what in reality is only a new form of slavery.'

Pope John Paul II, address in the Phoenix Park, Dublin (29 September 1979).

'On my knees, I beg you to turn away from the paths of violence and to return to the ways of peace. You may claim to seek justice. I, too, believe in justice, and seek justice. But violence only delays the day of justice. Further violence in Ireland will only drag down to ruin the land you claim to love and the values you claim to cherish.'

Pope John Paul II, address in Drogheda (29 September 1979).

'Young people of Ireland, I love you: Young people of Ireland, I bless you.'

Pope John Paul II, address in Ballybrit Racecourse, Galway (30 September 1979).

'That is an interesting theological principle.'

Gay Byrne, television personality and broadcaster, on hearing of the recommendation by priest that viewers should withhold television licence fees in protest at his interview with retired brothel-keeper, Madam Sin (8 November 1982).

'Surely the most defenceless and voiceless in our midst are entitled to the fullest constitutional protection.'

Catholic hierarchy (29 March 1983).

'We are moving towards a Catholic constitution for a Catholic people.'

Tomás Mac Giolla (4 April 1983).

'If we travel this road we shall be setting the scene for an increase in venereal diseases, teenage pregnancies, illegitimate births and even abortion.'

Dr Kevin McNamara, Bishop of Kerry (2 September 1984).

'There was a campaign to get [me] out, and [I have] no doubt that the Catholic Hierarchy are involved at the highest level. The campaign had been talked about at polite dinner parties.'

Barry Desmond TD (6 October 1985).

'Unless we are careful to check this fanatical politics, by the end of the century, genuinely Catholic social expression will have been pushed out of many areas.'

Dr Jeremiah Newman, Bishop of Limerick (November 1985).

'I'm not sure if I'll be telling them how to vote but they'll be under no illusions about the way I would like them to vote.'

Dr Jeremiah Newman, Bishop of Limerick (5 May 1986).

'If we remain the last Catholic country in Western Europe, that is because we have been remote, rural and poor: all these things are passing.'

Cardinal Tomás Ó Fiaich (24 August 1986).

'The right to life of the unborn does not appear to be on the government's agenda at the present time.'

Catholic hierarchy (14 April 1992). Quoted in Seán Duignan, *One Spin on the Merry-Go-Round* (1995).

'An accusation in today's Ireland is the equivalent of guilt.'

Fr Pádraig Mac hAol, *The Irish Times* (6 February 2006).

'I was carried away on gossamer wings.'

Annie Murphy, announcing details of her affair with Bishop of Galway Eamon Casey to a stunned listenership on RTÉ Radio 1's *Morning Ireland* (8 May 1992).

'There stood the Bishop, my love, without clerical collar or crucifix or ring, without covering of any kind. The great showman had unwrapped himself. Christmas of all Christmasses. This was for me more of a wonder than all the lark song or heather scents of Ireland. He stood before me, his only uniform the common flesh of humanity. He looked forlorn, almost like a child lost in a dark wood. I witnessed a great hunger. This was an Irish famine of the flesh.'

Annie Murphy, *Forbidden Fruit: My Life with Eamon Casey* (1993).

'I acknowledge that Peter Murphy is my son and that I have grievously wronged Peter and his mother, Annie Murphy.'

Dr Eamon Casey, Bishop of Galway (11 May 1992).

'I just got on the phone and all the seventeen years of anger blew in his face. I told him you had your chances and no more chances, and I said I'm going to come up there [to Galway] at Easter and pull your damn hat off.'

Annie Murphy (9 May 1992).

'Wear a condom — just in Casey.'

T-shirts sold in Dublin after Bishop Casey admitted he had kept secret the fact that he was a father.

'I intend to devote the remainder of my active life to work on the missions. In this way and with the help of God I will continue my lifelong commitment to the Church and its people.'

Dr Eamon Casey, Bishop of Galway, resignation statement after the discovery that he had fathered a child to Annie Murphy (6 May 1992).

'We have so many of our Church leaders caught up with a false ecumenism that they are afraid of saying the wrong thing, for fear of giving offence to the red-hatted weasel in Armagh.'
Revd William Hoey (23 August 1995).

'If the NHS was acceptable to Catholic bishops in Northern Ireland, what was morally wrong with something similar on this side of the border?'
Frank Cremin, Professor of Theology in Maynooth College, quoted in *The Irish Times* (3 November 2001).

'What is legally permissible rapidly comes to be seen as morally acceptable.'
Cardinal Cahal Daly, Primate of Ireland, speaking on divorce and abortion (9 October 1992).

'Desmond Connell may know a lot about angels but he knows fuck all about fairies.'
Senator David Norris, responding to a statement on homosexuality by the Archbishop of Dublin.

'"Anything in the paper this morning, Julia?" "Nothing, Mary, only the Pope is trying to make peace." "God forgive him, it's a wonder he wouldn't mind his own interference. It's enough to make you turn Protestant".'
Brendan Behan, *Brendan Behan's Island: An Irish Sketchbook* (1962).

'At that time ,there was great fear of the power of the clergy,. that if they disobeyed the clergy some blight or curse would befall them.'
Sean Cloney, Catholic farmer whose marriage to a Protestant

was to result in the Fethard boycott, speaking on *The Gay Byrne Show* (December 1998).

'It's quite true that I received such complaints. It is untrue, however, to say I did nothing about them.'

Bishop Brendan Comiskey, answering criticism of his handling of sex abuse allegations in Ferns diocese (2005).

'There were two different Fr Fortunes: the priest who would go up to the altar and give terrific sermons about the evils of drink, sex and sin and the other one who would talk to young boys about homosexuality, interview them one by one, and abuse them.'

Victim of clerical sex abuse, quoted in Alison O'Connor, *A Message from Heaven: The Life and Crimes of Father Seán Fortune* (2000).

Civil Servants

The first government departments were handed over on the 15 January 1922; others followed in December 1922, and the rest on 1 April 1923. But there was no doubt who the real bosses were, under the old administration or the new. And how come so many of them came from Kerry?

'In the main, civil servants own and run politicians. Given our multi-seat, proportional representation system of government, it cannot be otherwise.'

Frank Dunlop, *Yes Taoiseach: Irish Politics from Behind Closed Doors* (2004).

'I have come into knowledge of matters of national concern. I am afraid that if I follow the normal course the information might not reach the Government. Does my duty end with informing my Minister or am I responsible to the Government by whom I am appointed?'

Peter Berry, Secretary of Department of Justice, asking advice of President de Valera when his minister, Micheál Ó Móráin,

did not pass on information about the arms plot on to
Taoiseach Jack Lynch (20 April 1970). Quoted in Dick Walsh,
The Party: Inside Fianna Fáil (1986).

'Even a cursory glance at some leading civil servants in the
Free State reveals the wide scatter of their origins and, if
anything, the predominance of small town and rural Ireland
in their backgrounds.'
J.J. Lee, *Ireland 1912–1985: Politics and Society* (1989).

'Ministers do not write budget speeches, we do. Well, we
have in the past.'
Michael G. Tutty, Department of Finance official, on being
presented with the first draft of Ruairi Quinn's budget speech
(2 January 1995). Quoted in Ruairi Quinn, *Straight Left: A
Journey in Politics* (2005).

'There is no country in which sham excuses, political and
religious, for appointing incompetent men to responsible
posts flourish more signally than in Ireland.'
John Pentland Mahaffy, quoted in W.B. Stanford and R.B.
McDowell, *Mahaffy: A Biography of an Anglo-Irishman*
(1971).

'A few fellows drawing stamps were caught working by an
inspector in Tourmakeady and that will take a bit of squaring.
It all depends on the inspector. Some of the young inspectors
are tricky but they learn the ropes quick enough when they
learn about promotion. 'Tis easy to bluff them, though I have
met a few recently who don't care about hog, dog or devil.
Independent fellows. The sooner they learn that this world
cannot afford independent thinking the better. If every fellow

was thinking independently, we would have an nice rumpus to deal with. You'd never get anything done and no man would be safe in his bed.'

John B. Keane, *Letters of a Successful TD* (1967). The letters are said to have been based on those of Irish revolutionary Austin Stack. Much of the plot of the book refers to the TD's War of Independence record and his defence of his heroism in the Battle of Glenalee, which didn't exist.

'Ah, when all is said and done, he's someone's rearing after all, he could be worse, he could be a screw or an official from the Department.'

Brendan Behan, *The Quare Fellow* (1955).

'Everlasting typist in the Department of Enterprise and Employment.'

Translation of title of 'Permanent Secretary of the Department of Enterprise and Employment' during a visit to Tokyo (1994). Quoted in Ruairi Quinn, *Straight Left: A Journey in Politics* (2005). The title was changed to 'Secretary-General' the following year.

'Since the Freedom of Information Act, civil servants write their comments on post-it notes that can be removed if the main memorandum has to be made available for public viewing.'

Frank Dunlop, *Yes Taoiseach: Irish Politics from Behind Closed Doors* (2004).

'It wasn't a mistake, when in fact the whole pattern, in the vast bulk of boards, I don't want to make any further comment on that, I don't want to say, had been, that there wasn't. So, please, and I know with, with the best will in the world and you ask a question like that, Joe, was it a mistake, I don't want to see a statement tomorrow on radio or television, me adopting a word that you've used. I mean, cos, that's why, the reason why I wanted, I've given straight my position. Please report, I know you will because, please report me for what I say, not by way of responding to what is the question that's put to me. That's all. I think that will all emerge in time. I have no reason at all, at all, at all, and the government made it very, I want full disclosure, total and full disclosure, total and full disclosure. I can say this for myself and my department and my department is clearly. I am totally and ...'

Michael O'Kennedy TD, replying to a question from RTÉ's Joe O'Brien on whether a civil servant should have been put on the Greencore Board, quoted in Gene Kerrigan, *A Great Little Nation* (1999).

'While you cannot see the pig, you can see there is something wiggling in there. This is a poke with nothing in it but air, so far as one can judge. There is no sign of life at all in it.'

John Kelly, on the National Enterprise Agency, quoted in John Fanagan (ed.), *Belling the Cats: Selected Speeches and Articles of John Kelly* (1992).

'If you enter any of the hired and expensive warrens where the state's apparatchiks are housed, the accents you will hear on the telephones in active control of your destinies, whether of high rank, and thus probably male, or of low, and therefore more likely to be female, will be indubitably rural. The Irish people, in brief, have voted with their feet. The dwellers in the most beautiful of rural surroundings have deserted them for elsewhere. Those that did not have the option of the capital, the rural proletariat, went to Birmingham, Leeds,

Bradford, et al; but those that had the requisite political pull, knowledge of typewriting or talent for passing examinations flocked into Dublin.'

Anthony Cronin, *An Irish Eye: Art for the People*? (1985).

'There is someone here in this city who needs to have his head examined. What man knows for certain that there were 767,200 ducks in the country in 1956 and there are 337,000 in the country today? It is time there was an end to this codology. I do not mind civil servants sitting in an office having a soft time trying to cod the public, but they will not cod me.'

Joe Leneghan TD, Dáil Éireann (25 November 1963).

Michael Collins

Amid a revolution led by writers and orators, Collins was the handsome young hero, the one destined to be the subject of a Hollywood film. No politician since has ever come close to creating a legend to compare with his. Pity he had to die a premature death to complete the heroic tragedy.

'When will it all end? When can a man get down to a book in peace? I want peace and quiet. I want it so much I'd die for it.'
Michael Collins (November 1920).

'Nothing additional remains to be said. That volley which we have just heard is the only speech which it is proper to make above the grave of a dead Fenian.'
Michael Collins, at funeral of republican Thomas Ashe (30 September 1917).

"I found out that those fellows [British agents] we put on the spot were going to put a lot of us on the spot, so I got in first.'
Michael Collins (21 November 1920).

'Any scheme of government which does not confer upon the people of Ireland the supreme, absolute and final control of all of this country, external as well as internal, is a mockery and will not be accepted.'
Michael Collins (1 December 1918).

'The sooner fighting is forced and a general state of disorder created throughout the country the better it will be for the country.'
Michael Collins (March 1919).

'England will give us neither as a gift. The same effort that would get us Dominion Home Rule, will get us a republic.'
Michael Collins (August 1920).

'There is no crime in detecting and destroying in wartime the spy and the informer. They have destroyed without trial. I have paid them back in their own coin.'
Michael Collins (attrib.).

'Let us drop talking and get on with our work.'
Michael Collins (7 December 1920).

'Big Fellow! We'll see who's the Big Fellow!'
Eamon de Valera, on returning from the USA and hearing praise of the 'Big Fellow' (22 December 1920). Quoted in Tim Pat Coogan, *Michael Collins* (1991).

'No one is going to shoot me in my own country.'
Michael Collins (1 January 1922).

'The long hoor won't get rid of me that easily.'

Michael Collins, when requested by Eamon de Valera to go to the USA (18 January 1921). Quoted in Tim Pat Coogan, *Michael Collins* (1991).

'When I saw you before I said that the same effort that would get us Dominion Home Rule would get us a republic. I am still of that opinion . . . Compromises are difficult and settle nothing.'

Michael Collins (2 April 1921).

'Once a truce is agreed and we come out in the open it is extermination for us if the truce should fail. We shall be like rabbits coming out from their holes.'

Michael Collins (26 June 1921).

'Bring me into the spotlight of a London conference and it quickly will be discovered the common clay of which I am made. The glamour of the legendary figure will be gone.'

Michael Collins (20 August 1921).

'It was a good price, £5,000. Look at me: £625 dead or alive! How would you like that?'

Winston Churchill, to Michael Collins (20 November 1921).

Frederick Smith: 'I have signed my political death warrant.'

Michael Collins: 'I may have signed my actual death warrant.'

Casual conversation after the signing of the Anglo-Irish Treaty, Smith was talking about the Treaty being politically unacceptable to England's ruling class. Collins' words were to

gain greater significance after his assassination eight months
later (6 December 1921). Quoted in Tim Pat Coogan, *Michael
Collins* (1991).

'In my opinion it gives us freedom, not the ultimate freedom
that all nations desire and develop to, but the freedom to
achieve it.'
Michael Collins, on Anglo-Irish Treaty (19 December 1921).

'With equitable taxation and flourishing trade our North-East
countrymen will need no persuasion to come and share in the
healthy economic life of the country.'
Michael Collins, *The Path to Freedom* (1922).

'We've been waiting 700 years, you can have seven minutes.'
Michael Collins, on being told by the last Viceroy of Ireland
Edmund FitzAlan-Howard that he was seven minutes late in
arriving to take over Dublin Castle (16 January 1922).

'When countries change from peace to war, or war to peace,
there are always elements that make for disorder and that make
for chaos. If we could form some kind of joint committee to
carry on. I think that is what we ought to do.'
Michael Collins (7 January 1922).

'Think what I have got for Ireland? Something which she has
wanted these past 700 years. Will anyone be satisfied with the
bargain? Will anyone? I tell you this – early this morning I
signed my death warrant. I thought at the time how odd, how
ridiculous – a bullet may just as well have done the job five
years ago.'
Michael Collins, on signing the Anglo-Irish Treaty (December 1921).

'How could I ever have expected to see Dublin Castle itself – that dread Bastille of Ireland – formally surrendered into my hands by the Lord Lieutenant in the brocade-hung council chamber, on my producing a copy of the London Treaty?'

Michael Collins (16 January 1922).

'I am in sympathy with the majority of the IRA. The "big" businessmen and the politicians will come forward when peace is established and perhaps after some years gain control. Their methods will never demand a renewal of war.'

Michael Collins (3 April 1922).

'If the so-called Government in Belfast has not the power nor the will to protect its citizens, the Irish Government must find means to protect them.'

Michael Collins, after the sectarian killing of the MacMahon family by members of the new police force in Northern Ireland (9 April 1922).

'The safety of the nation is the first law and henceforth we shall not rest until we have established the authority of the people of Ireland in every square mile under their jurisdiction.'

Michael Collins (29 June 1922).

'There can be no question of forcing Ulster into union with the twenty-six counties. I am absolutely against coercion of that kind. If Ulster is to join us it must be voluntarily. Union is our final goal, that is all.'

Michael Collins (30 June 1922).

'The greatest oak in the forest had crashed; it seemed as if it must destroy all life in its fall. It did destroy the Sinn Féin movement and all the high hopes that were set in it, and a whole generation of young men and women for whom it formed a spiritual centre.'

Frank O'Connor, *The Big Fellow: Michael Collins and the Irish Revolution* (1937).

'I'd send a wreath but I suppose they'd return it torn up.'

Michael Collins, on death of former comrade Harry Boland (3 August 1922).

'So tear up your mourning and hang up your brightest colours in his honour; and let us all praise God that he had not to die in a snuffy bed of a trumpery cough, weakened by age, and saddened by the disappointments that would have attended his work had he lived.'

George Bernard Shaw, letter to Michael Collins' sister, Johanna (24 August 1922).

'There is one weapon that the British cannot take away from us: we can ignore them.'

Michael Collins, scripted in Neil Jordan's film adaptation of his life, *Michael Collins* (1995).

'Sold out.'

Sign in cinema for 1995 film *Michael Collins*. To which graffiti artist added: 'Michael Collins did not sell out.'

'Ah, whatever happens, my own fellow countrymen won't kill me.'

Michael Collins (attrib.) (18 August 1922).

'Then some film makers came from Hollywood to do a movie on the life and times of Michael Collins. They wanted a Pancho Villa. They needed a Pancho Villa — murderous, treacherous, wenching and stenching, a-sexual, b-sexual, c-sexual, x-y-ze-sexual, drunked, flunked and debunked, valued and devalued, signed, sealed and delivered. They said no. We said no. So Mr Director went home and got fired. End of film.'

Patrick J. Twohig, *The Dark Secret of Béalnabláth* (1991).

Corruption

How we came to trust them in the first place is a complicated story. What is interesting is that the electorate were ahead of the tribunals – they got their chance to vote out the councillors and TDs against whom allegations were made, and took it. Apart from the ones who went on to top the poll, of course.

'Why is the harp the national symbol of Ireland? It is because you have to pull strings to play it.'

Brendan Behan (attrib.)

'As a politician he took the usual line, bellowing that he was a patriot first and foremost, that he would never do anything save for the good of his country and would therefore be a thorn in the side of the government. In other words, he was announcing that he was for sale.'

John Donovan, *Evening Press* journalist and historian describing of eighteenth-century politician John Giffard, Dublin.

'Meath has more pensioners than any other county in Ireland.'
Michael Clery TD, Dáil Éireann (5 December 1929).

'Whereas the local people may have been corrupt in
twopenny-halfpenny matters, the Ministry are corrupt in
matters of hundreds of thousands of pounds.'
Frank Aiken TD, in Dáil Éireann (17 June 1931).

'Laois-Offaly's answer to the Locke tribunal leaves no doubt
as to belief in existence of corruption.'
Oliver J. Flanagan, telegram to Eamon de Valera after topping
the poll in the general election, in the aftermath of the
Locke's distillery tribunal (1951).

'Do not be dispirited if at some time people in high places
appear to have low standards.'
George Colley TD (April 1967).

'When, as happened recently, a government minister
considers it necessary to refer publicly to the apparently low
standards of integrity of those in high places, it is clear that we
are faced with something more than normal, irresponsible
rumour-mongering. The only people in high places are Fianna
Fáil.'
Liam Cosgrave (9 May 1967).

'There was a situation that had arisen where I had taken
some cocaine during the few hours before which made me
panic and to leave my room and to look for security. When
security arrived I wasn't at all happy that these were regular
security men. I was on the balcony of a seventeenth floor
hotel room. I was fighting in my mind for my survival and

that's why I was staying in public view. I can blame no one, only myself. No, I am not a cocaine user. In a weak moment I took the goddamn stuff and in no way am I looking for pity.'

Ben Dunne, businessman (23 February 1992).

'The standards governing the conduct of ministers are, and must be, more stringent than those which cover the conduct of private people. They must stand above suspicion. They must not place themselves in the way of adverse comment.'

Terence O'Neill, Prime Minister of Northern Ireland, after dismissing Minister for Agriculture Harry West for urging the opening of an airport in which he had a financial interest (26 April 1967).

'The lobbies and corridors of the House were seething with rumours of corruption on housing in Dublin city, of men who had become very rich at the expense of the local authorities and the poor. Certain people in high places are in possession of information which is not available to the individuals most concerned. We have the racketeers and the privateers closely associated and prominently identified, hidden behind the scenes of the now-famous association called Taca.'

Paddy Harte TD, Fine Gael (27 April 1967).

'I am a firm and convinced believer in jobbery. Any time I hear of a Fianna Fáil minister being criticised for putting their friends into jobs, I am angered because I am not in the same position to put my friends into jobs.'

Oliver J. Flanagan TD, on *The Late Late Show* (1968).
Quoted in T. Ryle Dwyer, *Nice Fellow: A Biography of Jack Lynch* (2001).

'If the present Dáil carried any flavour at all it was the smell of death and corruption in every sense of the word since the events of May 1970 [the Arms Crisis]. So low is the status of politics that if every one of us was led off to internment in the Blasket Islands, in the words of Cromwell, not a dog would bark.'

David Thornley TD (16 December 1971).

'Moral indignation and breast-beating on their part is quite sickening considering that they drove the former President Ó Dálaigh from office. These are not high standards, but double standards.'

Seamus Brennan TD (31 October 1990).

'That is a sorry list and indeed an incomplete list of low standards in high places.'

Peter Barry TD (4 November 1982).

'£10,000 reward fund for information leading to conviction or indictment of a person or persons for offences relating to a land re-zoning in the Republic of Ireland.'

Michael Smith, former chairman of An Taisce, and Colm Mac Eochaidh, barrister, an advertisement placed in *The Irish Times* (3 July 1995).

'I did not make a secret of the fact that Dunnes Stores paid me for professional services by way of assistance towards my house. If someone were trying to hide income, would he or she not be more likely to put it in an offshore account?'

Michael Lowry TD, after resigning amid allegations of corruption (12 December 1996).

'Well if you think I'm bad, there's another fellow got a million.'

Michael Lowry TD, on day of resignation (1996).

'I never took money from anyone to do a political favour as far as planning is concerned.'

Padraig Flynn TD, on *The Late Late Show* (15 January 1999).

'Oh yeah. Haven't seen him now for some years. He's a Sligo man. Went to England. Made a lot of money. Came back and wanted to do a lot of business. Didn't work out for him. He's not well. His wife's not well. And he's out of sorts.'

Padraig Flynn TD, on *The Late Late Show* when asked if he knew businessman Tom Gilmartin. As a result of this statement, Gilmartin appeared at the Flood Tribunal to back up allegations of corruption against Flynn (1999).

'You guys make the Mafia look like monks.'

Tom Gilmartin, businessman, to politicians he met, having given Padraig Flynn £50,000 to secure planning permission for developments on Bachelor's Walk, Dublin, and Liffey Valley, Dublin.

'I would not have that man consulting on a shithouse.'

Tom Gilmartin, replying to the suggestion he had employed Liam Lawlor as a consultant.

'Mr James Gogarty told me that JMSE wished to make a political contribution to me and I received from him in good faith a sum of £30,000 as a totally unsolicited political contribution. At no time during our meeting was any favour sought or given.

I did not do any favours for or make any representations to anyone on behalf of JMSE. I have done nothing illegal, unethical or improper. I find myself the victim of a campaign of calumny and abuse.'

Ray Burke TD, statement after allegations of corruption were made against him (7 August 1997).

'You must understand that, political donations to political parties or to individuals, there's nothing illegal about that. There never was.'

Padraig Flynn TD (January 1998).

'I don't think there was a whole lot said, but I said, "Will we get a receipt for this money?" and Bailey said, "Will we fuck!"'

James Gogarty, businessman and controller of building company JMSE, at the Flood Tribunal (19 January 1999).

'Am I to believe that no politician had any association with anything that happened during that decade? It's news to me.'

Maurice Doyle, a former senior civil servant and Governor of the Central Bank, to the Public Accounts Committee of the Dáil investigating bogus non-resident accounts (September 1998).

'I was a very heavy saver and over the years I made investments of various sorts.'

George Redmond, former Assistant City and County Manager, attempting to explain how, on a take-home salary of £19,000, he managed to lodge £265,000 in 1988 and 1989 and had net investments totalling £660,000.

'For lawful power is still superior found / When long driven back, at length it stands the ground.'

Mr Justice Thomas Smyth, quoting lines from Dryden's *Absalom and Achitophel* when sentencing Liam Lawlor TD for contempt of court and failing to co-operate with the investigations of the Flood Tribunal (1 February 2002).

'I am not protecting anyone, only myself.'

Liam Lawlor TD, in an interview with RTÉ's Charlie Bird (4 February 2002).

'I'll go into a deep sulk.'

Charlie McCreevy TD, on what would happen if Fine Gael wouldn't meet his deadline to open their accounts to independent analysis (13 May 2002).

'The sordid side of the country's secret life is now under the spotlight and we are deeply challenged by the emergence of so many difference forms of evidence.'

Mary McAleese, President (2000).

'It is an essential part of the machinery of democracy that people should be prepared to support in this voluntary way the party whose policy appears to them to be in the best interests of the country.'

Taoiseach Jack Lynch defending Fianna Fáil fund-raising arm Taca (December 1968).

'Tribunal news demoralises, shakes confidence in politics and even destabilises the State. All politicians and public offices are smeared and held up to public odium.'

Des Hanafin, politican (2000).

'What has he against me? Is it because I didn't pull the state solicitorship for his son? How could I do that and he an opposition man?'

John B. Keane, *Letters of a Successful TD* (1967).

'This whole State is alive with hoodlums and politicians, and when was there any difference between these two classes?'

Flann O'Brien, *Stories and Plays* (1973).

'The capacity of businessmen to subscribe to political parties is closely related to the principle of free speech.'

Charles J. Haughey (15 July 1997).

'It grew organically, as part of the maturing of the economy through the 1980s. People with shared financial and sometimes political interests formed alliances and looked after one another. Another level of society had its trade unions and tenants' organisations. The golden circles are looser, the connections are through social, banking, financial, political and professional networks. Common interests are recognised, backs are scratched. It is seldom that favours are sought or given: few have to stoop so low. Mostly, people in these circles know the right thing to do.'

Gene Kerrigan and Pat Brennan, *This Great Little Nation: The A-Z of Irish Scandals and Controversies* (1999).

Liam Cosgrave

The seventh Taoiseach was, amazingly, the first Fine Gael leader to get the top job and probably the only premier in world history to vote against his own government in a division. His most memorable sound bites came when he departed from his script. He should have done it more often.

'I don't know whether some of you do any hunting or not, but some of these commentators and critics are now like mongrel foxes; they are gone to ground and I'll dig them out and the pack will chop them when they get them.'

Liam Cosgrave, departing from prepared script at Fine Gael Ard Fheis (20 May 1972).

'I now solemnly reaffirm that the factual position of Northern Ireland within the United Kingdom cannot be changed except by a decision of a majority of the people of Northern Ireland.'

Liam Cosgrave (13 March 1974).

'The Taoiseach has behaved like an idiot, but one thing he has succeeded in doing is getting himself into the Guinness Book of Records.'

David Thornley, Labour TD on the decision by Taoiseach Liam Cosgrave to vote against his own government's Contraception Bill, helping defeat it by seventy-five votes to sixty-one (20 July 1974).

'The Government believes the extent of violent crime by irregular, subversive, terrorist bodies and the further threat to the institutions of the State implied by events, constitute a national emergency affecting the vital interests of the State.'

Liam Cosgrave (31 August 1976).

'Not for the first time has this party stood between the people of this country and anarchy. And remember, those people who comment so freely and write so freely – some of them aren't even Irish . . . Some of these are blow-ins. Now as far as we're concerned they can blow out or blow up.'

Liam Cosgrave, Fine Gael Ard Fheis (21 May 1977).

'Dying for Ireland, as usual.'

Liam Cosgrave, commentating on a Fianna Fáil speaker in the Dáil.

Coups and Shaftings

The end of the Civil War meant a change of methods, not intent, for the assassins who hang around in Irish politics. The spirit of Béal na mBláth was alive and well in the corridors of Leinster House..

'A vote of confidence is a sure sign you are in trouble.'
Patrick Hillery, quoted in Stephen Collins, *The Power Game: Fianna Fáil since Lemass* (2000).

'Those responsible for the debacle have no option but to take the honorable course open to them. I think there is some dissatisfaction about the leadership at the moment.'
Charles J. Haughey, speaking after his acquittal on arms charges (23 October 1970).

'I do not want any deputy to go into the lobby with me to buy time, because I am not in the business of buying or selling time.'
Jack Lynch, to parliamentary party meeting (October 1970).

'You know you are the worst fucking judge of people I have ever met.'

Seán Doherty to Charles J. Haughey, after Jack Lynch resigned as party leader and Haughey assumed he would win by a large vote (5 December 1979). Quoted in Dick Walsh, *The Party: Inside Fianna Fáil* (1986).

'I don't buy my colours coming out of the stadium.'

Jim Tunney, on his public backing for George Colley in the Fianna Fáil leadership contest (11 December 1979). Quoted in Ken Whelan and Eugene Masterson, *Bertie Ahern* (1998).

'What's the difference between a caucus and a cactus? All the pricks are on the outside of a cactus.'

Ben Briscoe (attrib.), on Fianna Fáil caucus meeting to remove Jack Lynch as leader (10 July 1979).

'For the reasons I have outlined it will be obvious to the house that neither I nor my colleagues can vote confidence in the Government at the conclusion of this debate.'

Dick Spring, pulling Labour out of the 1992–4 Coalition (November 1994).

'Shot on my estate this morning.'

Note accompanying two ducks delivered to Martin O'Donoghue days after Charles J. Haughey had sacked him as Minister for Economic Planning.

'A majority of the parliamentary party has, it seems to me, changed the traditional Fianna Fáil rule and legitimised the withholding of loyalty to, and support for, the elected leader. I very much regret this but I am a realist and I accept it.'

George Colley, in a statement as Tánaiste in Haughey's first government.

'The Irish people need some leadership and it is not being supplied.'

Charlie McCreevy, proposing an attempt to remove Charles J. Haughey (27 December 1981).

'They took me for granted. That was the mistake they made last night. It might seem pompous for me to say it, but I feel I was entitled to influence the Government more than I did.'

Jim Kemmy (27 January 1982).

Ben Briscoe: 'I love you, Charlie.'

Charles J. Haughey: 'I love you too, Ben.'

David Andrews: 'I hope the papers don't hear about this.'

Exchange at Fianna Fáil parliamentary party meeting in which Haughey survived a leadership challenge (27 January 1983). The remarks were published in the following morning's *Irish Press*.

'There is a unity of purpose now that hasn't been there since Charlie took over. We have a united party again.'

Albert Reynolds, after Desmond O'Malley's expulsion from Fianna Fáil (26 February 1985).

'I have today tendered my resignation as Tánaiste and Minister for Defence in order to enable the Government to continue with its successful programme. The decision is mine and mine alone. I have not been subject to pressure from any quarter.'

Pre-prepared resignation statement handed to Brian Lenihan by Charles J. Haughey (26 October 1990).

An Ceann Comhairle: 'We will now resume on the Derelict Sites Bill, 1989.'

Michael O'Kennedy: 'There are some derelict sites around now.'

Aftermath of government defeat on the Haemophiliacs Bill which brought an end to the 1987-9 Government (26 April 1989).

'Lest there be any doubt about what is at stake here, I can't contact my Tánaiste. He will not speak to me.'

Charles J. Haughey, to a Fianna Fáil party meeting (27 October 1990). Quoted in Stephen Collins, *The Power Game: Fianna Fáil since Lemass* (2000).

'Don't burst the party, Albert.'

Gerry Collins, television interview (7 November 1991).

'Country and Western, I think they are called.'

Charles J. Haughey, on his opponents within Fianna Fáil after the leadership bid by Albert Reynolds and revelations by Seán Doherty (21 January 1992).

'Albert is being hung for the wrong crime.'

Charlie McCreevy (16 November 1994).

'Pee Flynn would be doing himself a disservice if he did not support the motion to discontinue the leadership forthwith of Charles Haughey.'

Padraig Flynn, referring to himself in the third person as he addressed a meeting to decide on Charles J. Haughey's leadership of Fianna Fáil (9 November 1991). Haughey survived by fifty-five votes to twenty-two. Quoted in Stephen Collins, *The Power Game: Fianna Fáil since Lemass* (2000).

'We have nothing to fear from our enemies without. It is the enemies within we must fear.'

Charles J. Haughey, to colleagues before his resignation as Fianna Fáil leader and Taoiseach (22 January 1992).

'We have come for a head. Harry's or yours. It doesn't look like we are getting Harry's.'

Ruairi Quinn to Albert Reynolds (16 November 1994).

Maire Geoghan Quinn: What are you looking for, Dick?

Dick Spring: I think it's all over.

Exchange (16 November 1994). Quoted in report of *Select Committee on Legislation and Security*.

Eamon de Valera

When they put a mathematician in charge of the country, they didn't expect the equation to go on so long. Even after his death, the debate continued. People who weren't born in his lifetime get fired up by the mention of his name. His reputation comes up for discussion every couple of years, every time another part of Irish identity gets debated. As brand names go, Dev was a winner for fifty years. It is hard to find anyone to admit it nowadays, but maybe that too will change.

'Arguing with de Valera is like trying to catch a man on a merry-go-round, or picking up mercury with a fork.'
David Lloyd-George, on trying to pin down de Valera (January 1922). Quoted in Deirdre McMahon, *Republicans and Imperialists: Anglo-Irish Relations in the 1930s* (1984).

'Why doesn't he try a spoon?'
De Valera's reply. Quoted in Deirdre McMahon, *Republicans and Imperialists: Anglo-Irish Relations in the 1930s* (1984).

'I was reared in a labourer's cottage here in Ireland . . . and whenever I wanted to know what the Irish people wanted, I had only to examine my own heart and it told me straight off what the Irish people wanted.'

Eamon de Valera, in reply to a jibe at his 'foreignness' in the *Freeman's Journal* (6 January 1922).

'Let Ulster Unionists recognise the Sinn Féin position which has behind it justice and right. It is supported by nine-tenths of the Irish people and if those Unionists do not come in on their side, they will have to go under.'

Eamon de Valera, during the Clare by-election (5 July 1917).

'I have read the speeches of the honourable member for East Clare [de Valera]. They are not excited, and so far as language is concerned they are not violent. They are plain, deliberate, and I might also say, cold-blooded incitements to rebellion.'

David Lloyd-George, British Prime Minister in House of Commons (23 October 1917). Quoted in Dorothy Macardle, *The Irish Republic* (1951).

'England pretends it is not by the naked sword, but by the good will of the people of the country that she is here. We will draw the naked sword to make her bare her own naked sword.'

Eamon de Valera (25 October 1917).

'It [partition] is after all only an old fortress of crumbled masonry – held together with the plaster of fiction.'

Eamon de Valera, draft speech for South Armagh by-election (January 1918).

'They [the Unionists] are a rock in the road. They must make up their minds not to be peddling with this rock. They must if necessary blast it out of their path.'

Eamon de Valera, speech in South Armagh (27 January 1918). Quoted in John Bowman, *De Valera and the Ulster Question* (1982).

'We are not doctrinaire republicans.'

Eamon de Valera (15 October 1917). Quoted in Tim Pat Coogan, *De Valera* (1993).

'The blossoms are not the fruit but the precursors of the fruit – beware how you pluck them.'

Eamon de Valera, on proposed negotiations with the British (4 May 1921).

'We most earnestly desire to help in bringing about a lasting peace between the peoples of these two islands, but see no avenue by which it can be reached if you deny Ireland's essential unity and set aside the principle of national self-determination.'

Eamon de Valera, letter to David Lloyd-George (28 June 1921).

'No offer will be accepted by the nation if that offer deprives us of the essentials of freedom. Now, it is a hard thing to know what are the essentials of freedom. Freedom is a thing that you cannot cut in two – you are either all free or you are not free. It is, therefore, for complete freedom that we are struggling, and we tell everybody that this nation will continue to struggle for its freedom until it has got the whole of it.'

Eamon de Valera, Limerick (5 October 1921).

'There can be no question of our asking the Irish people to enter an arrangement which would make them subject to the British king. If war is the alternative, we can only face it.'

Eamon de Valera (24 October 1921).

'The terms of this agreement are in violent conflict with the wishes of the majority of this nation. I cannot recommend the acceptance of this Treaty. The greatest test of our people has come.'

Eamon de Valera, rejecting Anglo-Irish Treaty (8 December 1921).

'I am against this Treaty, not because I am a man of war, but a man of peace. I am against this Treaty because it will not end the centuries of conflict between the two nations of Great Britain and Ireland.'

Eamon de Valera (18 December 1921).

'We were elected by the Irish people, and did the Irish people think we were liars when we said that we meant to uphold the Republic? I am against this Treaty because it does not reconcile Irish national aspirations with association with the British Government.'

Eamon de Valera (19 December 1921).

'I stand as a symbol for the Republic. Neither publicly nor privately have I lowered that position. It would be a matter for impeachment if I did. I didn't go to London because I wished to keep that symbol of the Republic pure even from insinuation, or even a word across the table that would give away the Republic.'

Eamon de Valera, Dáil Éireann (4 January 1922).

'We have had a glorious record for four years; it has been four years of magnificent discipline in our nation.'
Eamon de Valera, after the Dáil approved the Treaty
(7 January 1922).

'If they accepted the Treaty, and if the Volunteers of the future tried to complete the work the Volunteers of the last four years had been attempting, they would have to complete it, not over the bodies of foreign soldiers, but over the dead bodies of their countrymen. They would have to wade through, perhaps, the blood of some of the members of the Irish Government in order to get Irish freedom.'
Eamon de Valera (17 March 1922).

'I am safe in saying that if the [Republican] Army were ever to follow a political leader, Mr de Valera is the man.'
Rory O'Connor (13 April 1922).

'Young men and young women of Ireland, the goal is at last in sight. Steady all together; forward, Ireland is yours for the taking. Take it.'
Eamon de Valera after the seizure of the Four Courts (16 April 1922).

'I told them not to do it, even pleaded with them, but they wouldn't listen to me, and now what will become of us all.'
Eamon de Valera (attrib.), in Tim Pat Coogan, *Michael Collins* (1991) after the shooting of Collins.

'The day Michael Collins was shot, where was de Valera? Ask the people of Béal na Bláth and they will tell you.

There was a scowling face at a window looking out over that lovely valley and de Valera could tell you who it was.'

Revd Jeremiah Cohalan, Canon of Bandon (September 1922).

'We can best serve the nation at this moment by trying to get the constitutional way adopted.'

Eamon de Valera, letter to Liam Lynch (7 February 1923).

'For our part, we are content to rest for the moment, if it must be so, simply faithful.'

Eamon de Valera, speech at Bodenstown (21 June 1925).

'I would disappoint a number here if I were not to start by saying, "Well, as I was saying to you when we were interrupted."'

Eamon de Valera, in Ennis, where he was arrested a year previously at public meeting (15 August 1924).

'Once the admission oaths of the twenty-six-county and six-county assemblies are removed, it becomes a question not of principle but of policy whether or not Republican representatives should attend these assemblies.'

Eamon de Valera (10 March 1926).

'At the bidding of the English, Irishmen are today shooting down, on the streets of our capital, brother-Irishmen, old comrades-in-arms, companions in the recent struggle for Ireland's independence and its embodiment – the Republic [. . .] England's threat of war – that, and that alone – is responsible for the present situation.'

Eamon de Valera, after the attack on the Four Courts (28 June 1922).

Soldiers of the Republic, Legion of the Rearguard: the Republic can no longer be defended successfully by your arms. Further sacrifice of life would now be vain, and continuance of the struggle in arms unwise in the national interest and prejudicial to the future of our cause. Military victory must be allowed to rest for the moment those who have destroyed the Republic. Other means must be sought to safeguard the nation's right.'

Eamon de Valera (24 May 1923).

'The question is raised whether this oath is really an oath in the theological sense. For me it is enough that it is called an oath officially and it begins with "I do solemnly swear" and that, whenever it suits, it will be held to be an oath by those who impose it and will be so understood by the world.'

Eamon de Valera (16 May 1926).

'Another objection raised is that entering a twenty-six-county assembly would be an acceptance of partition. I deny that. To recognise the existence of facts, as we must, is not to acquiesce in them.'

Eamon de Valera, inaugural address to Fianna Fáil party (16 May 1926).

'The required declaration is not an oath . . . it is merely an empty political formula which deputies can conscientiously sign without becoming involved, or without involving their nation, in obligations of loyalty to the English Crown.'

Eamon de Valera, before entering Dáil Éireann (10 August 1927).

'I am putting my name here merely as a formality to get the permission necessary to enter among the other Teachtaí that were elected by the people of Ireland. You must remember that I am taking no oath.'

Eamon de Valera, after entering Dáil Éireann (11 August 1927).

'A servant in a big mansion must give up the luxuries of a certain kind which were available to him by being in that mansion . . . If he goes into the cottage he has to make up his mind to put up with the frugal fare of that cottage.'

Eamon de Valera (12 July 1928). Quoted in J.J. Lee, *Ireland 1912-1985: Politics and Society* (1989).

'All history is a record of man's efforts to realise ideals. We in Ireland are suffering bitterly from the false ideals that have been imposed on us. We retain however, great reserves of spiritual strength and true idealism.'

Eamon de Valera (5 February 1929). Quoted in Philip Hannon and Jackie Gallagher (eds), *Taking the Long View: 70 Years of Fianna Fáil* (1996).

'If the British Government should succeed in beating us in this fight, then you could have no freedom, because at every step they could threaten you again and force you again to obey the British. What is involved is whether the Irish nation is going to be free or not.'

Eamon de Valera, during the Economic War (8 November 1932).

'The narrow, Celtic limits of his vision had left his twin ideal of a united and Gaelic Ireland not only unfulfilled but further away than ever. De Valera was an austere and ageing figure from the past whom the public revered as a national monument but regarded as irrelevant to the contemporary scene. With the conspicuous exception of Princess Grace of Monaco, the level of foreign representation at the funeral was probably not as high as the Irish people might have hoped.'

J.T. Hickman, British Ambassador in Dublin, after de Valera's death in 1972.

'You sometimes hear Ireland charged with a narrow and intolerant Nationalism, but Ireland today has no other hope than this; that, true to her holiest traditions, she should humbly serve the truth and help by truth to save the world.'

Eamon de Valera, opening radio transmission in Athlone (6 February 1933).

'Let us remove these forms one by one, so that this state that we control may be a republic in fact and that when the time comes, the proclaiming of the Republic may involve no more than a ceremony, the formal confirmation of a status already attained.'

Eamon de Valera at speaking at Arbour Hill (23 April 1933). Quoted in Maurice Moynihan, *Speeches and Statements by Eamon de Valera 1917-73* (1980).

'Do you know that ever since 1921 the main purpose in everything I have done has been to try and secure a base for national unity?'

Eamon de Valera, letter to Joe McCarrity (31 January 1934).

'De Valera brought to a fine art the process of acting constitutionally while cloaking his actions in revolutionary rhetoric.'

Tim Pat Coogan, *De Valera* (1993).

'The stormy petrel. The fiery cross of Irish politics.'

Seán Ó Faoláin, on Eamon de Valera.

'Either Dev is to be judged as a visionary or a fixer but never as what he was, a fascinating mixture of both, which sought the benefits of modernity and the liquidation of its costs.'

Declan Kiberd, quoted in Philip Hannon and Jackie Gallagher (eds), *Taking the Long View: 70 Years of Fianna Fáil* (1999).

'The man who did his damnedest to cut the country's throat and now invited it to commit political hara-kiri in order to save his face.'

Kevin O'Higgins (1927).

'The Spanish onion in the Irish stew.'

J.H. Thomas, British Dominions Secretary, describing de Valera, quoted in Deirdre McMahon, *Republicans and Imperialists: Anglo-Irish Relations in the 1930s* (1984).

'He is on the border line between genius and insanity. I have met men of many countries and have been governor of a lunatic asylum, but I have never met anybody like [him] before.'

Lord Granard (25 August 1934).

'Stop making love outside Áras an Uachtaráin.'

Paul Durcan, poet, imagined reproach from de Valera to modern Ireland around him.

'To have failed to call upon the German representative would have been an act of unpardonable discourtesy to the German nation and to Hempel himself. During the whole of the war, Dr Hempel's conduct was invariably correct – in marked contrast with Gray. I certainly was not going to add to his humiliation in the hour of defeat.'

Eamon de Valera, letter to Robert Brennan, Irish envoy to Washington, defending much-criticised decision to pay condolences at German legation on the death of Hitler.

'As long as our own country or any part of it is subjected to force, the application of force, by a stronger nation, it is only natural that our people, whatever sympathies they might have in a conflict like the present, should look at their own country first.'

Eamon de Valera (2 September 1939).

'The Government have been faced with the alternative of two evils. We have had to choose the lesser, and the lesser evil is to see men die, rather than that the safety of the whole community should be endangered.'

Eamon de Valera, refusing to release IRA prisoners on hunger strike (9 November 1939).

'Mr Churchill is proud of Britain's stand alone, after France had fallen and before America entered the war. Could he not find in his heart the generosity to acknowledge that there is a small nation that stood alone, not for one year or two, but for several hundred years, against aggression; that endured spoliations, famines, massacres in endless succession; that was clubbed many times into insensibility, but that each time, on returning consciousness, took up the fight anew; a small nation that could never be got to accept defeat and had never surrendered her soul?'

Eamon de Valera, reply to Winston Churchill (17 May 1945).

'The Taoiseach's broadcast reply to Mr Churchill was as
temperate as it was dignified. Mr de Valera has his faults as a
statesman and as a politician; but he has one outstanding
quality. He is a gentleman.'
The Irish Times (18 May 1945).

'The voice of the Irish gentleman, Spanish grandee, was a
welcome relief from the chorus of retaliatory rancour and
self-righteousness then deafening us. Eamon de Valera comes
out of it as a champion of the Christian chivalry we are all
pretending to admire.'
George Bernard Shaw, on Churchill–de Valera exchange.

'We had him on a plate. We had him where we wanted him.
But look at the papers this morning!'
John Kearney, Canadian High Commissioner in Dublin (18
May 1945).

'Phrases make history here.'
John Maffey, British representative, in letter to London on
reaction to Churchill–de Valera exchange (21 May 1945).
Quoted in Robert Fisk, *In Time of War* (1985).

'Look up any standard book of reference and get from any of
them any definition of a republic, any description of what a
republic is, and judge whether our state does not possess
every characteristic mark by which a republic can be
distinguished or recognised.'
Eamon de Valera (17 July 1945).

'A small country like ours that had for centuries resisted
imperial absorption, and that still wished to preserve its

separate national identity, was bound to choose the course of neutrality in this war. The continued existence of partition, that unnatural separation of six of our counties from the rest of Ireland, added, in our case, a further decisive reason.'

Eamon de Valera, radio broadcast to USA (17 March 1941).

'I wish there was some way of knowing who will win this war. It would make decisions much easier.'

Eamon de Valera (attrib.), remark in private conversation during the Second World War.

'There is a cultivated myth that would have us believe that De Valera won elections by putting on a big black cloak, appearing on platforms at twilight illuminated by blazing sods of turf, and casting spells in bad Irish.'

Breandán Ó hEithir, *The Begrudger's Guide to Irish Politics* (1986).

'A Dhomhnall, I have to tell you, you are abolished.'

Eamon de Valera (attrib.), to Domhnall Ó Buachalla announcing he was abolishing the position of Governor General.

'I have to tell you, you are another one.'

Ó Buachalla's reply, quoted in Breandán Ó hEithir, *The Begrudger's Guide to Irish Politics* (1986).

'The Fianna Fáil crowd recognised but the one true Pope, by the name of Eamon de Valera, late of 42nd Street.'

Brendan Behan, *After the Wake* (published posthumously, 1981).

'Well, I've always heard that de Valera is a wonderful man. They say he's fluent in seven languages. More's the pity we can't understand him once in a while.'

Brendan Behan, *The Hostage* (1958).

'I would remind you that I have just as much contempt for a bully standing or seated.'

Eamon de Valera, quoted in Seán Ó Faoláin, *The Life Story of Eamon de Valera* (1933).

'If there is one British thing the Irish have always learned to fear, and with good reason, it is British diplomacy.'

Seán Ó Faoláin, *The Life Story of Eamon de Valera* (1933).

'You can arrest father, but you will never make English of us!'

Vivion de Valera, quoted in Seán Ó Faoláin, *The Life Story of Eamon de Valera* (1933).

'I would vote for him if it meant having to starve.'

Clarewoman speaking during Economic War, quoted in Seán Ó Faoláin, *The Life Story of Eamon de Valera* (1933).

'"He is the saviour of our country, the greatest Irishman since Saint Patrick." "But Saint Patrick wasn't an Irishman," I protested. "Neither was Dev," he whispered triumphantly.'

John B. Keane, *Letters of a Civic Guard* (1976).

'In May 1944, a minor provision of the Transport Bill (more nationalisation) was defeated when two Independent deputies voted against the Government.

Their names were Cole and Byrne and they fuelled many a joke in the pages of Dublin Opinion. De Valera had a quick look into his heart before driving up to Áras an Uachtaráin in the middle of the night to dissolve the Dáil; he almost precipitated a Presidential Election such was the shock to Douglas Hyde's ageing nervous system.'

Breandán Ó hEithir, *The Begrudger's Guide to Irish Politics* (1986).

James Dillon

The only party leader to be expelled by his own party, Dillon would have made a great Taoiseach, but the greatest orator of his time never made it beyond Minister for Agriculture and leader of Fine Gael at a time when they missed power by an agonisingly narrow margin. Maybe he wouldn't have wanted it any other way.

'As so often happens in this unhappy country, the provocative insolence of British politicians gets the colour of vindication by things we in our folly do.'

James Dillon, speaking on the Constitution (Removal of Oath) Bill, Dáil Éireann (27 April 1932).

'The war is over. It is now becoming a question of accountancy.'

James Dillon, Dáil Éireann (26 February 1936).

'I want to recall with pride that we fought a desperate battle for the preservation of free speech in this country and let it never be forgotten that we could not have won the battle but for the Blueshirts who helped us win it. And as they fought they were fighting not for party but for democracy, and democracy won. No thanks to those who were opposed to it.'

James Dillon, former Fine Gael leader, statement on the anniversary of the foundation of party and Blueshirt connection (1983).

'We are living under a sword of Damocles that might fall to destroy freedom and man's right to adore God . . . It may be policy of this government to stand neutral, but I am not neutral. The issue at stake means whether I want to live or die.'

James Dillon, Dáil Éireann (10 February 1941).

'I say today that the German Nazi Axis seeks to enforce on every small nation in Europe the same beastly tyranny that we successfully fought for 700 years.'

James Dillon, Dáil Éireann (17 July 1941).

'We may see a sovereign, independent and united Ireland delivered from the nauseating frauds of a dictionary republic sooner than we anticipate.'

James Dillon, Dáil Éireann (18 February 1948).

'Our people will get the government they vote for. If it is 'Animal Farm' they want, they should vote for Fianna Fáil, but if it is democracy and decency they want, I suggest they will have to look elsewhere. I think the acceptance of corruption as the norm in public life is shocking. Why pretend that in this island of saints and scholars there is no corruption and bias, if it has come to be accepted as the norm?'

James Dillon, Dáil Éireann (13 April 1967).

'The Minister was going over to America to settle world affairs, having of course settled the agricultural problem here. As a matter of fact there is a story told that during the voyage there was a Question Time and the compère asked, "Who is the greatest man the world ever produced?" One very good looking gentleman, a very honest man, said, "James Dillon." The compère asked: "How do you know James Dillon is the greatest man the world ever produced?" and the answer was, "I am James Dillon." '

M.J. Davern (19 May 1949).

'I thought of suing them for copyright, but it had this distinction – it was the inter-party programme, with Annie Oakley's addition: "Anything they can do, we can do better."'

James Dillon, Dáil Éireann (15 November 1951).

'The first real Irishman I have ever met.'

Louella Parsons, syndicated American columnist (1961).

'When the choice lies between dishonour and material ruin on the one hand and the risk of war upon the other, terrible as that risk may be, frightful as the consequences may be of facing it, I think a nation with our traditions should face that risk of war and refuse to submit to a blackmail of terror designed to make it sell its honour and stake its whole material future on the vain hope that it may be spared the passing pain of effort now.'

James Dillon, Dáil Éireann (17 July 1941).

'I do not think that rational people have any doubt that, in ten years' time, no transatlantic passenger plane bound for the

Continent of Europe or Great Britain will stop at Shannon, and if there was nothing but passenger traffic scheduled for Rineanna in ten years' time we would have nothing in Rineanna but rabbits. It is more than likely that Rineanna will be a deserted wilderness in ten years' time.'

James Dillon, Dáil Éireann (12 February 1947).

'Day-old chicks were known in the Gaeltacht as "Dillons bheaga" (Little Dillons).'

Breandán Ó hEithir, *The Begrudger's Guide to Irish Politics* (1986).

Economists, Tigers and Other Animals

Life would be much easier for politicians if they didn't have to worry about making the economy work for the rest of us. For decades, they screwed it up. And when it came right, and they went around looking for the credit for making it right, they were surprised when we refused to believe them.

'The dismal science.'

Charles J. Haughey on economics.

'The collapse and discredit of the whole Fianna Fáil concept of a quarter of a century, which has been founded on the idiotic heresy of economic self-sufficiency and derived from the days when we thanked God the British market was gone forever and hoped that a day might dawn when no ship would sail the seven seas so that we might be more prosperous in our isolation.'

James Dillon (1 August 1961).

'I heard the late Archbishop of Tuam mention a pleasant observation of somebody's: that Ireland would never be happy until a law were made for burning anything that came from England, except their people and their coals.'

Jonathan Swift, *A Proposal for the Universal Use of Irish Manufacture* (1720).

'The worst case of all is to be bad and to be poor after it all.'

Eamon de Valera, speaking during the Treaty debates.

'Blythe had a financial policy. He had virtually no economic policy, beyond the act of faith that prosperity would follow from fiscal rectitude.'

J.J. Lee writing about the 1920s Minister for Finance Ernest Blythe, in *Ireland 1912–1985: Politics and Society* (1989).

'You can't corral the people in, you can't pass a bill that says you can't emigrate.'

Eamon de Valera (1948).

'After independence we were so pleased with ourselves for having kicked the Brits out that it was a while before we noticed that, having taken over the country, we now had the job of running it.'

Gene Kerrigan, *Never Make a Promise You Can't Break: How to Succeed in Irish Politics* (2002).

'The Irish people are falling into a mood of despondency. After thirty-five years of native government, can it be, they are asking, that economic independence achieved with such sacrifice should wither away?'

T.K. Whitaker (1957).

'In other countries governments rose and fell on their competence in dealing with the economy. Here we didn't need an economy. We had emigration.'

Gene Kerrigan, *Never Make a Promise You Can't Break: How to Succeed in Irish Politics* (2002).

'The Government was a shyster debtor: grave injury had been done to the economic and social fabric of the State: the country was so much worse. The Government is dooming the Irish people to go down with the British ship.'

Seán MacEntee, the Fianna Fáil finance spokesman, on devaluation, in the *Sunday Press* (13 November 1949).

'You are the only one in the Cabinet who understands the problem or is capable of understanding the problem.'

T.K. Whitaker, to Minister for Finance Gerry Sweetman (1956).

'To accelerate progress by strengthening public confidence after the stagnation of the 1950s, indicating the opportunities for development and encouraging a progressive and expansionist outlook. In order to achieve these aims we must be prepared to take risks under all headings, social, commercial and financial, if we are to succeed in the drive for expansion.'

T.K. Whitaker, *Programme for Economic Development* (November 1958).

'It was the first time a political party had decided to spend its way out of a boom.'

Charlie McCreevy, on the 1977 Fianna Fáil election manifesto.

'We regard them as part of a global generation of Irish people. We shouldn't be defeatist or pessimistic about it. After all, we can't all live on a small island.'

Brian Lenihan, on emigrants (12 October 1987).

'While the Government may not be worried the parents of these young people are. These people have made great sacrifices to educate their children and it is madness for the benefits of this to be made available to another economy.'

Peter Barry (12 October 1987).

'An Bord Snip.'

Nickname of Expenditure Review Committee introduced by the 1987–9 government.

'The Asgard List.'

Nickname of spending options presented to the government in the 1980s and repeatedly rejected, the scrapping of the sail-training vessel the *Asgard* was a regular item.

'Doheny & Nesbitt's School of Economics.'

Reference to the Economic Consensus on State Matters which was apparently formulated in a public house on Baggot Street, a short distance from Leinster House (1986).

'We are in danger of moving from the Celtic Tiger to the Celtic Ostrich.'

David McWilliams (30 October 1998).

'It's the economy, nitwit.'

Mary Harney, responding to Bertie Ahern in a Clintonesque phrase (23 April 2002).

'Doheny & Nesbitt's is frequented by an eclectic mixture of politicians past their sell-by dates, journalists looking for gossip, economists of a mostly left-wing variety, poseurs and pseuds.'

Frank Dunlop, *Yes Taoiseach: Irish Politics from Behind Closed Doors* (2004).

Education

The poets and schoolteachers who led the revolution were not the first to realise that classrooms can be very political places. Their legacy was Ireland's own version of class conflict. Teachers filled the parliamentary benches for generations afterwards. Did education fuel the boom? Is the teacher a tiger? Anyone who went to school before the 1970s probably have the marks to prove it.

'I thank the goodness and the grace / That on my birth have smiled / And made me in these Christian days / A happy English child.'

Verse by Richard Whately, Archbishop of Dublin, which was to be recited daily in Irish national schools around 1910.

'An education system which more wickedly does violence to the elementary human rights of Irish children than would an edict for the general castration of Irish males. One of the most terrible things about the English education system in Ireland is its ruthlessness. I know no image for that ruthlessness in the natural order. The ruthlessness of a wild beast has a certain mercy – it slays. But this ruthlessness is literally without pity and without passion.'

Padraig Pearse, *The Murder Machine* (1916).

'The spirit of the shoneen to which allusion is made is propagated largely through certain sports that are regarded as peculiarly the privilege of wealthy classes and belong to a British tradition. If we have a large influx into the colleges of the National University from schools in which this shoneen spirit prevails, it will be very hard, in fact exceedingly hard, to preserve the Gaelic tradition.'

Professor William MaGennis (16 November 1922).

'Educate, educate, educate.'

James Warren Doyle, Bishop of Kildare and Leighlin, paraphrasing Daniel O'Connell (1835).

'The salaries vary according to classification, but in all cases are not only too meagre to attract the best talent to the profession but are insufficient to enable the teacher to live even in frugal comfort. Classification depends mainly on average attendances and owing to the large number of schools with low averages due to the absence of an efficient, or indeed any, system of enforcing attendance, half of the teachers can never rise above the lowest grade.'

Catherine M. Mahon, President of the Irish National Teachers Organisation (INTO), *Leabhar na hÉireann* (1922).

'Notwithstanding the long and expensive course of training which is necessary, secondary teachers are the worst-paid body of workers in Ireland. So wretchedly inadequate are the salaries that many of them are forced to work long and hard after ordinary school hours in order to be in a position to supply themselves and their families with the ordinary necessaries of life. As well as this, a teacher has no guarantee, particularly if he is attached to a Catholic school, of anything in the way of security of tenure, and the controllers of the Catholic schools persist in their determination not to give him any guarantee, regarding him, in fact, as no more than a casual labourer, whose services should be dispensed with as soon as a clerical teacher is available.'

L.G. Murray, President of ASTI, *Leabhar na hÉireann* (1922).

'The mind, spirit and outlook of Dublin Castle percolates down to the teachers and the schools through the medium of the Inspectors, Organisers, Staffs and Training Colleges. Teachers must take their cue from inspectors regarding the tone and outlook of their teaching, else they can be made to suffer in a multiplicity of ways. Inspectors in their turn must take their cue from the education office, failing which they are likely to suffer in the matter of promotion and pension. In the partial success of the National System in anglicising the youth of Ireland it has acquired an unpleasant flavour. In its partial failure it has become the subject of indifference and perhaps contempt.'

Catherine M. Mahon, President of the INTO, *Leabhar na hÉireann* (1922).

'Trinity College, having the politics of the average Irish Protestant, is metaphorically, and indeed even literally, an English fortress. When the Irish Protestant aristocracy had its glorious summer of patriotism in the eighteenth century, Trinity College shone in the glow. It has shared the moral decay that came upon its class after the union, though as late as 1848 it could still produce Protestant patriots, of whom it is almost ashamed. But it could never make anything of the Catholics who entered it, except complacent lawyers.'

Arthur E. Clery, *Leabhar na hÉireann* (1922).

'Belfast University has, with the exception of one brilliant work, contributed little to the intellectual life of the country. It suffers greatly from its habit of importing Britishers to fill its teaching posts. Ambitious only to change their place of exile, they are too often birds of passage, and in the result there is lack of continuity in its university life.'

Arthur E. Clery, *Leabhar na hÉireann* (1922).

'The Clongowes boys left office and the Christian Brothers boys came in.'

Seán Lemass, on the transfer of power from Cumann na nGaedhael to Fianna Fáil in 1932.

'Clongowes contains the cream of Ireland – rich and thick.'

James Dillon (attrib.).

'There was no realisation of the importance of education in the modern world and there was certainly no evidence of this outburst of enthusiasm for education which is so characteristic now.'

'Seán Lemass Looks Back', *Irish Press* (4 February 1969).

'Christian Brother education was an effective mechanism for social advancement and transformation. It was particularly well adapted to the circumstances of the urban poor and still is today. The Brothers were the educators of the State's public servants, its teachers and administrators, its priests, technocrats and business entrepreneurs. Their primary schools, established in almost every Irish town by the late 1950s, educated the vast majority of the tax-bearing, mainly urban and male populations. In the post-Lemass years, this emerging cadre of skilled and productive workers, in whom the Christian Brother primary-school education had instilled a form of practical and civic patriotism, served well a nation transitioning from a rural and agricultural base towards a broad-based manufacturing economy.'

Michael Murray, Christian Brothers province leader (6 June 2005).

'What the fuck are we going to do about free education?'

Donogh O'Malley, to Secretary of the Department of Education Seán Ó Conchubhair, quoted in Christina Murphy, 'How O'Malley Launched Free Scheme', *The Irish Times* (10 September 1986).

'I propose from the coming school year, beginning in September of next year, to introduce a scheme whereby up to the completion of the Intermediate Certificate course, the opportunity for free post-primary education will be available to all families.'

Donogh O'Malley, Education Minister, speaking in Dun Laoghaire, announcing free secondary education without prior consultation with Cabinet (10 September 1966)

'Dear Donogh, I think I should tell you straightaway that your speech regarding free secondary education on Saturday night last must not be considered by you to involve any commitment on the part of the government, or the provision of additional money for education services in the coming or any other year. You will of course appreciate that if other ministers in respect of their own work were to seek to commit the government by making speeches in advance of the approval of the government of their plans, everything would become chaotic.'

Seán Lemass, letter to Donogh O'Malley (12 September 1966, released in 1996).

'For present and future generations of Irish children he broadened the horizons of knowledge and enhanced their prospects of life.'

Jack Lynch, funeral oration for Donogh O'Malley (March 1968).

'No one is going to stop me introducing my scheme next September. I know I am up against opposition, and serious organised opposition, but they are not going to defeat me on this.'

Donogh O'Malley (9 February 1967).

'Parents who wish to bring up their children in a Christian way must chastise them in a parental way when necessary. Many parents were guilty of grave neglect in that respect. In childhood the least sign of anger, untruthfulness or disobedience must not go unpunished. The rod must be used whenever the child refuses to obey father or mother. Young children especially have no respect for anything else. Let the child feel the rod, it is the best food he could have.'

Lawrence Gaughran, Bishop of Meath, Lenten Pastoral just before his death in 1928.

'Dear Taoiseach, I believe that it is essential for a government from time to time to propound bold new policies which both catch the imagination of the people and respond to some widespread, if not clearly formulated, demand on their part. I believe also that you have on a number of occasions done precisely this when it was needed. If I was under a misapprehension in believing that I had your support for my announcement, I must apologise. I would hope, however, that what I have said will persuade you that I was right in making it and that you will give me your full support in getting my plans approved by the government.'

Letter by Donogh O'Malley, letter to Seán Lemass (14 September 1966). Described as one of the best letters ever written by a government minister in Ireland by Diarmaid Ferriter, *What If? Alternative Views of Twentieth Century Ireland* (2006).

'Every year, some 17,000 of our children finishing their primary-school course do not receive any further education. This is a dark stain on the national conscience, for it means that some one third of our people have been condemned – the great majority through no fault of their own – to be part-educated, unskilled labour, always the weaker who go to the wall of unemployment or emigration.'

Donogh O'Malley (14 September 1966).

'It would be unreasonable for me to forbid the teacher to adopt any deterrent that might be adopted by a just and wise parent, and a just and wise parent might on occasion deem it necessary to inflict an adequate amount of corporal punishment in order to control the child and bring him up in the way he should go.'

Patrick Hillery (4 May 1961).

Elections and the Electorate

No wonder politicians worry. They don't like elections and managed to fool us into not having them for a long time. As late as 1919, a quarter of parliamentary seats were not contested and the tradition of agreed candidates continued right up to 1969 in Northern Ireland. Today, the politicians maybe no better, but at least we now have the pleasure of voting them out every few years.

'The agony and the ex-TD.'

Ben Briscoe, after the long count for a seat between himself and Eric Byrne (1992).

'Election contests between Fine Gael and Fianna Fáil came down to one thing: who loved Ireland the most.'

Michael Mills, *Hurler on the Ditch: From Journalist to Ombudsman* (2005).

'Like being at your own post-mortem without the anaesthetic.'
Ruairi Quinn, on the stress of election counts, quoted in
Ruairi Quinn, *Straight Left: A Journey in Politics*

'There are a few fellows around here who will be looking for
oil for their bicycle chains.'
Jackie Healy-Rae, indicating he is about to withdraw support
for the Government (2002).

'The country is mad. It seems to constantly produce and
reproduce these outrageous situations. And I think it's partly to
do with the fact that we elect loads of loonies, these characters
who open their mouths and insert both feet in them.'
Gerry Stembridge, *Scrap Saturday* writer, quoted in Stephen
Dixon and Deirdre Falvey, *Gift of the Gab: The Explosion in
Irish Comedy* (1999).

'We must not always judge of the generality of the opinion by
the noise of the acclamation.'
Edmund Burke, *Letters on a Regicide Peace* (1796).

'It was an incredible exercise in professionalism, scheduling,
publicity, press relations, stage management, the lot. I came
back and said to myself if it will work out there, why won't
it work here? It wasn't easy to persuade people back home
that it would work.'
Seamus Brennan, Director of Elections for Fianna Fáil's most
successful election in 1977, on how he had borrowed from
Jimmy Carter's presidential election campaign in 1976.
Quoted in T. Ryle Dwyer, *Nice Fellow: A Biography of Jack
Lynch* (2001).

'Politicians are the product of the people, and the values that the people hold. And a lot of other people would be equally good at the job. And there is the matter of being the right man in the right street at the right time.'

Mairin Lynch, wife of Jack Lynch, to journalist Stephen O'Byrnes during the 1977 election campaign. Quoted in T. Ryle Dwyer, *Nice Fellow: A Biography of Jack Lynch* (2001).

'Considering the electorate we have, the politicians are very good actually.'

Garret FitzGerald, quoted in Katie Hannon, *The Naked Politician* (2004).

'The electorate don't know where their number three preferences go.'

Seán Lemass, arguing against proportional representation (1959).

'If tomorrow we found ourselves in the charge of a junta of colonels up from the Curragh, how many people would take to the barricades in defence of the Dáil?'

John Kelly TD (12 June 1971).

'Bolandised.'

Reference to the redrawing of constituency boundaries to favour Fianna Fáil for the 1969 general election.

'I know the hat size of every one of my constituents.'

Oliver J. Flanagan (attrib.). Flanagan used to pick up hats from Clery's department store for constituents on the way back to his Laois-Offaly constituency.

'Tullymander.'

Reference to the redrawing of constituency boundaries to favour Fine Gael and Labour for the 1977 general election.

'The reverend mother circuit.'

John Mulcahy, editor of *Hibernia,* describing Jack Lynch's election campaign of 1977.

'Vote early and often.'

Slogan attributed to several people. William Norton, leader of the Labour Party, 1932–63, used it to sign off election speeches.

Charles J. Haughey. 'Oh of course, give it to the O'Connors. Have it fixed somehow.'

P.J. Mara: 'Yes Boss, but which O'Connor, Pat?'

Charles J. Haughey. 'No, give it to the other O'Connor, Pat.'

Sketch on satirical radio programme *Scrap Saturday,* scripted by Owen Roe, Gerry Stembridge and Dermot Morgan (1990).

'It's showtime again.'

P.J. Mara, at the launch of the 2002 election campaign.

'It's the bins, stupid.'

Noel Whelan, explaining Joe Higgins' enormous popularity after his election for Dublin West (17 May 2002).

'The operation of gerrymandering is never a very pretty spectacle . . . and it really reaches the nadir of absurdity and disruptiveness when we have a map erected in the Custom House with members of the Fianna Fáil party gathered round it like bees or wasps round a honey pot.'

James Dillon (1961).

'Pat O'Connor is an example to us all. Too many people in these sorry days are contemptuous of the ballot box and prefer to strike, protest or demonstrate instead of casting their vote. What this country needs is twice as many Pat O'Connors.'

Gene Kerrigan, in *Magill* magazine, after Charles J. Haughey's election aide was found to have voted twice in the 1982 election.

'I want to satisfy the man who lies in a settle bed in the West or the South of Ireland, who comes in from a hard day's work and who likes to hear a varied programme from his Irish station.'

James Everett, Minister for Posts and Telegraphs (12 July 1949).

'That old cliché, the triumph of hope over experience, is what keeps our democracy going. You might call it a confederacy of reluctant cynics.'

Frank Dunlop, *Yes Taoiseach: Irish Politics from Behind Closed Doors* (2004).

'There are people in this country of the devoutest faith who would be reluctant to thieve or lie, but who will go in with the utmost cheerfulness to thieve or lie when they get inside a polling booth.'

Darrell Figgis, speaking on Prevention of Corrupt Practices at Elections Bill, Dáil Éireann (20 October 1922).

'The function of an election manifesto is to get you elected. Therefore, it should contain nothing negative and nothing that annoys any significant percentage of the voters.'

Gene Kerrigan, *Never Make a Promise You Can't Break: How to Succeed in Irish Politics* (2002).

'We'll just strike terror into the heart of the Irish people, won't we?'

Seán Duignan's mischievous remark, quoted in the *Irish Independent* (1 May 1992).

'A wise electorate would assassinate the local TD. By-elections mean that projects that were stalled get new life and projects that would never be attempted get started.'

Katie Hannon, *The Naked Politician* (2004).

'The truth is that, as the disaffected and the disillusioned would have it, we get the politicians we deserve.'

Frank Dunlop, *Yes Taoiseach: Irish Politics from Behind Closed Doors* (2004).

'Too much should not be read into the reactions of tired people after a long day at work.'

Michael McDowell, on exit polls (21 June 2004).

'Fine Gael is convinced it's the Red Chinese, and Fianna Fáil, being more intellectually mature, believes it's the Martians.'

Hugh Leonard, *Time Was* (April 1989).

'Dáil Éireann is the only place in Ireland where the Civil War is still going on.'

John B. Keane, *Many Young Men of Twenty* (1961).

'I wouldn't get many votes if I hung around the big shots. They would start saying that my success has gone to my head.'

John B. Keane, *Letters of a Successful TD* (1967).

'All of our candidates had been wiped out except Tom himself, who told the House that there were two united Irish parties, of which he was one.'

Maurice Healy, *The Old Munster Circuit: A Book of Memories and Traditions* (1939).

'Lenin said that one of his missions in life was to abolish the village idiot. It is just as well, for the sake of many of our pillars of rural democracy, that Comrade Lenin's writ never ran in Ireland.'

Breandán Ó hEithir, *The Begrudger's Guide to Irish Politics* (1986).

'For some members of the Government part at least of the motivation for this decision was a concern lest publication of data from such a census should raise the question of a further constituency revision that might undo the Tullymander. There could scarcely have been a worse moment to cancel the census.'

Garret FitzGerald, on the decision to cancel the census in 1976, *All in a Life* (1991).

Europe and Eurocrats

First there were six, and Ireland wasn't invited, then nine (including Ireland), ten, twelve, fifteen and twenty-five. And all of the newcomers had one question to ask: how did Ireland do it? And how exactly did Europe bring peace and prosperity to the island? Wish we knew the answer.

'My only programme for Ireland consists, in equal parts, of Home Rule and the Ten Commandments. My only counsel to Ireland is, that in order to become deeply Irish, she must become European.'

Thomas Kettle, *Apology* (1880-1916)

'We have no right to go into the EEC. We were never part of Europe and we never will be.'

John Bryans, Grand Master of Grand Orange Lodge (6 August 1971).

'The choice is between taking part in the great new renaissance of Europe or opting for economic, social and

cultural sterilisation. It is like that faced by Robinson Crusoe when the ship came to bring him back into the world again.'
Jack Lynch (5 May 1972).

'We have a thirty-two-county underdeveloped area. The people on both sides of the Border look forward to assistance and co-operation from Europe.'
Oliver J. Flanagan (11 March 1971).

'If we enter the Common Market, in two years there will not be a snail on our walls, a frog in our pools or a fish in our bays.'
Joseph Lenehan (10 July 1971).

'Today, we stand at a most important crossroads in our history.'
Jack Lynch, in Dáil Éireann (21 March 1972).

'We are too small and our tiny voice in the organs of government of the EEC can and will be drowned out.'
Brendan Corish, Labour Leader, at anti-EEC rally in Cork (5 May 1972).

'Willows are weak, yet they bind other wood.'
Irish Times editorial, accompanying news that a willow tree representing Ireland had been planted among nine trees on the canal to celebrate Ireland's accession to the European Economic Community (1 January 1973).

'The diminishing importance of London as a centre of decisions affecting Northern Ireland, many of which would in future be taken in Brussels, might reduce northern

Unionists' sensitivities on the issue of whether the remaining powers were exercised in Westminster or in Dublin.'

Garret FitzGerald (28 January 1972).

'Far from there being any contradiction between our demand for independence from Britain and our later accession to the EC, Irish membership of the EC ultimately justified that independence.'

Garret FitzGerald, *Reflections on the Irish State* (2003).

'Le tout ensemble chancing their arm.'

Description of an EU meeting in Paris (11 June 1993).
Quoted in Seán Duignan, *One Swing on the Merry-Go-Round* (1995).

Famous Last Words and Hostages to Fortune

Politicians don't like being reminded of what they said last week, especially when they come out with meaningless mantras like, 'a week is a long time in politics.' Sorry, guys and girls.

'The tyranny of consistency.'

Brian Lenihan, explaining why politicians change their mind on the RTÉ programme *Questions and Answers*.

'Ireland today is peaceful beyond record. She has almost entirely, I believe, cast aside her suspicions and her rancour toward this country; and England, on her side, is, I believe, today more willing than ever she was in her past history to admit Ireland on terms of equality, liberty and loyalty into that great sisterhood of nations that makes up the British Empire.'

John Redmond (16 April 1912).

'No decent Republican should ever enter the present Dáil.'
Eamon de Valera (25 January 1925).

'No longer shall our children, like our cattle, be brought up
for export.'
Eamon de Valera (19 December 1934).

'This country is no longer behind the times, nor is it to be
considered as second-rate or third-rate in any of its services.'
Alfie Byrne (19 May 1945).

'The repeal of the External Relations Act will take the gun
out of Irish politics and will give us complete independence
with a republican form of government.'
John A. Costello (14 November 1948).

'We should support the civil rights campaign in the North.
There is a majority there that wants unity with Britain and we
must respect that, but at the same time we must reject their
right to oppress the minority.'
Conor Cruise O'Brien (25 January 1969).

'Coalition set to take election.'
Irish Times front-page headline (16 June 1977). Fianna Fáil
captured 50.6 per cent of the vote and the biggest majority
ever won by any party in a general election.

'75 per cent poll to bring narrow election win for Coalition.'
The Irish Times front-page headline the following day.

'Haughey on brink of resignation.'
Irish Press, front-page headline (26 January 1983).

'I am glad to be an ally of Paisley's in the defence of the Union.'

Conor Cruise O'Brien (3 May 1998).

'The honeymoon period [is] coming to an end, but it has not ended in divorce or a stand-up fight between husband and wife. The troops have been accepted by both communities and a happy, comfortable married life is under way.'

Denis Healey, British Minister of Defence, on visit to Northern Ireland (19 September 1969).

'Let those who seek to dance on our graves dance lightly lest they waken the corpse.'

Eddie McAteer, last leader of the Northern Ireland Nationalist Party (23 November 1969).

'Internment has flushed out the gunmen.'

Brian Faulkner, Stormont Prime Minister (14 August 1971).

'I say to the Catholics of Northern Ireland, you have nothing to fear from the Army.'

Harty Tuzo, General Officer Commanding the British army in Northern Ireland, four weeks before Bloody Sunday (20 December 1971).

'Surely it was more dangerous to leave these people [the IRA] in the shadows? In a modern democracy, the autonomy of radio or television was as vital as the freedom of the press or of Parliament.'

Conor Cruise O'Brien (23 November 1972).

'I intend to take out Section 31 of the Broadcasting Act and remove altogether, and deprive any future minister of, the power to issue the kind of directions that we have.'

Conor Cruise O'Brien, Minister for Posts and Telegraphs, at ITGWU conference, promising to end legislation banning IRA and Sinn Féin interviews on RTÉ (8 June 1973).

'I am allowing the directive issued by my predecessor to stand ... I am determined to ensure as far as I can that while armed conspiracies continue to exist in this country, their agents shall not be allowed to use the state broadcasting system for a systematic propaganda effort.'

Conor Cruise O'Brien (25 April 1974).

'The Government was now using that interview as an excuse to destroy the independence of the RTÉ Authority and that was something that was totally unacceptable. The real threat to the country was not the IRA but the threat to freedom of speech.'

Garret FitzGerald (23 November 1972).

'How can [the Minister for Justice] come into this Parliament and ask it to support a Bill the like of which can only be found on the statute books of South Africa?'

Patrick Cooney, Fine Gael spokesman on Justice, opposing the Offences Against the State (Amendment) Bill which allowed wide government powers against subversive organisations (29 November 1972).

'For the first time in any part of Ireland, Protestant, Catholic and Dissenter will be working together to build a new society.'

John Hume, SDLP Deputy Leader, on the power-sharing agreement with Ulster Unionist and Alliance parties (22 November 1973).

'Refusal to enter coalition is a core value for Fianna Fáil.'

Padraig Flynn, in a radio interview broadcast while Charles J. Haughey was meeting Desmond O'Malley to strike a deal which would enable them to form a coalition government (3 July 1989).

'It's all right, I just haven't told them yet.'

Charles J. Haughey to Bobby Molloy on public statements that there would be no coalition. Quoted in Stephen Collins, *The Power Game: Fianna Fáil since Lemass* (2000).

'We will not act as a crutch for conservative parties in decline.'

Proinsias De Rossa (8 November 1992).

'Given these it must surely be considered amazing that any party would consider coalescing with Fianna Fáil. We will not support any government with the track record of this one.'

Dick Spring (5 November 1992).

'This will be a government that will stand and fall on the issue of trust. Let me make no mistake about that. If it does not conform to the highest standards of accountability and openness, it will cease to exist. It is as simple as that.'

Dick Spring (15 January 1993).

'The talks would set back the inter-community peace process very significantly and were in any event doomed to failure.'

Michael McDowell (26 April 1993).

'Coalition is completely ruled out. We went before the electorate on the basis that we wouldn't form a coalition. A majority of the people voted for a Fianna Fáil government and our position was always that if we hadn't an overall majority we would form a minority government.'

Charles J. Haughey, just before Fianna Fáil and the Progressive Democrats formed a coalition government (1 July 1989).

'The distinction between a wise silence and silent wisdom is like the distinction between the Minister for Agriculture's constitutionalism and my avowed unconstitutionalism.'

Seán Lemass, Dáil Éireann (28 May 1928).

Fianna Fáil

The history of Irish politics since 1932 has been whether the rest of the political parties could get their act together and elbow Fianna Fáil out of power. Each of the parties has had to reinvent itself to stay ahead of changing tastes; Fianna Fáil have been better at it than the others at every stage of the game, across rural and urban, artisan and cottier, business and professional. The party which got a name for building bridges has latterly been better known for just building. In the history of political spin, nobody has quite figured out exactly how it managed to increase its support while devastating agricultural income in the 1930s.

'1   Securing the political independence of a united Ireland as a republic.

2   The restoration of the Irish language and the development of a native Irish culture.

3   The development of a social system in which, as far as possible, equal opportunity would be afforded to

every Irish citizen to live a noble and useful Christian life.

4   The distribution of the land of Ireland so as to get the greatest possible number of Irish families rooted in the soil of Ireland.

5   The making of Ireland as an economic unit, as self-contained and self-sufficient as possible, with a proper balance between agriculture and other essential industries.'

Foundation aims of Fianna Fáil (16 May 1926).

'We must not allow ourselves to be hypnotised by our prejudices and feelings on the one hand or by our opponents' propaganda on the other. To underestimate our strength is even a worse fault than to overestimate it. We must not let our opponents dissuade us from attempting a task that is well within our power by suggesting it is impossible. We must, if we really want to succeed, endeavour to judge the situation just as it is, measure our own strength against it, lay our plans and then act with courage and intensity.'

Eamon de Valera, addressing the inaugural meeting of Fianna Fáil (16 May 1926).

'The party that was to end Partition, the party that was to halve taxation, the party that was to have every man sitting down under his own vine tree smoking a pipe of Irish-grown tobacco are not here today.'

Kevin O'Higgins, speaking in Dáil Éireann, commenting on the failure of Fianna Fáil to take up its seats (23 June 1927).

'They were dragged in kicking and screaming and praying

to God that their hands would wither before they ever signed the oath, and then they signed it. They came into this House a minority, and they got into this House as a minority through the instrumentality of proportional representation.'

James Dillon, Dáil Éireann (6 March 1968).

'Fianna Fáil is a slightly constitutional party. We are perhaps open to the definition of a constitutional party, but, before anything, we are a Republican party. Five years ago we were on the defensive and perhaps in time we may recoup our strength sufficiently to go on the offensive. Our object is to establish a Republican government in Ireland. If this can be done by the present methods we have, we would be very pleased. If not, we would not confine ourselves to them.'

Seán Lemass, Dáil Éireann (21 March 1928).

'I saw them come into this House with their pockets bulging with revolvers, and one old gentleman down in the lobby in the telephone box assembling a machine-gun. I see them now lolling on the Government benches in mohair suits.'

James Dillon, speaking in Dáil Éireann. This is the origin of phrase 'mohair suits' used to taunt Fianna Fáil (6 March 1968).

'Fianna Fáil: 'This lot are pragmatic, e.g. they will say or do anything that will get them into power.'

Gene Kerrigan, *Never Make a Promise You Can't Break: How to Succeed in Irish Politics* (2002).

'There is no crisis in Fianna Fáil, never was, and never will be.'

Sean Flanagan, during Arms Crisis (5 May 1970).

'I am firmly convinced that this is the juncture in the life of Fianna Fáil to make a complete break from the divisive contest campaigns within the party, because that system has not just worked for us.'

Bertie Ahern, on not entering the leadership race (1993).

'Fianna Fáil will survive. You can have Boland but you can't have Fianna Fáil.'

Patrick Hillery, to hecklers supporting Kevin Boland at the Fianna Fáil Ard Fheis (20 February 1971).

'Fianna Fáil in 1973 was a political party totally lost. At sea. Rudderless. There was little, if any, co-ordination in its stances of government policy or action. People who had been ministers and were accustomed to the trappings of office, instant advice from civil servants, prepared scripts and the like, found it difficult to operate politically on a TD's salary and therefore they reverted to their previous professions. The truth is that the party was suffering from what would be seen as post-traumatic stress and was in a time warp.'

Frank Dunlop, *Yes Taoiseach: Irish Politics from Behind Closed Doors* (2004).

'Wright asked me about all we had done. He found it hard to say co-op and could only say co-co-co until in the end he gave it a name he could say – "The Cope". That was the christening.'

Paddy the Cope Gallagher, *My Story* (1939).

Fine Gael

Fine Gael came within a few percentage points of Fianna Fáil for a brief period in the 1980s, helped by a weakened Labour Party and its command of issues of political corruption, a stable policy on Northern Ireland and a firm grip on the economy. Recapturing that share has become a bit of a target for the party since, as it passes through a revolving door of leadership changes. But politics moved on, and the party bears as little resemblance to that of the 1980s as it does to the more confessional era that went before.

'There was a time when execution was his method of putting his opponents aside.'

Michael Clery, on Richard Mulcahy in Dáil Éireann (17 June 1931).

'Fine Gael never seems to grasp that intellect is intimidating, so they continue to lack the common touch. The L and H boredom of summoning up previous malpractices of Fianna

Fáil (what I call in RTÉ training courses The Fatal Tyranny of Fine Gael Fact).'

Eoghan Harris, political communications strategist, quoted in Emily O'Reilly, *Candidate: The Truth Behind the Presidential Campaign* (1991).

'One cannot reconcile a period of prosperity with a period of civil war, or with a period in which ministers have to go about the country with their lives in their hands and revolvers in their pockets.'

R.S. Anthony, Dáil Éireann (3 April 1930).

'I do not expect any members of the front bench who were with us formerly, and who did the things that were done in 1921 and 1922, to have any regard for law or order.'

Eamon de Valera, Dáil Éireann (17 June 1931).

'People say give Dev enough rope and he will hang himself. We gave him enough rope and he hanged the rest of us.'

Michael Tierney, Fine Gael founding member (attrib).

'I'm greatly in favour of the fascist state.'

Patrick Hogan, Fine Gael founding member (attrib).

'The National Guard being a non-military or civil organisation there will be no military equipment of any kind. Blue is adopted as the organisation's colour for flags, shirts, ties, badges, etc. Just as sports clubs adopt a distinctive blazer or jersey. Any organisation may adopt a special colour without infringing the law.'

Eoin O'Duffy (21 July 1933).

'The Corporate State must come in the end, in Ireland as elsewhere. Its inauguration need not be the work of any one political party, but the future is with those who honestly, intelligently and fearlessly will undertake its cause.'

Michael Tierney, Fine Gael founder member, in *United Ireland* (16 December 1933).

'It is time for us to pull the wool off our eyes and tell this House and tell the country what industrialisation in this country really means. It means that we are handing this country over to a gang of international Jews.'

Paddy Belton (4 March 1937).

'Who owns the wealth of Dublin? Is it the Irish volunteers or the Irish people? No, it is not, but the rotten old Jews.'

Captain Patrick Giles (1 December 1937).

'I think it is a terrible thing that we, who call ourselves a Christian people, should stand idly by and allow the Jews, the Gentiles, the Freemasons and Communists to dictate the policy of the world. We stand for Christianity. We stand for it against the Jews, the Gentiles, the Reds and the Freemasons of the world. Let us show the world that we will lay down our lives before we will cower before the Red hordes of this world.'

Captain Patrick Giles (13 July 1938).

'We are asked to agree to this expenditure by the Minister for Defence who, at one time, thought that he was a super-Irishman. Today, he is nothing more than Britain's tool for the coming European war, engineered by the financiers and Jews of the world. We were England's tools for 700 years.

If we are going to be her tool in the coming war, then I say the devil mend us.'

Captain Patrick Giles (16 February 1939).

'How is it that we do not see any of these Acts directed against the Jews, who crucified Our Saviour nineteen hundred years ago, and who are crucifying us every day in the week? How is it that we do not see them directed against the Masonic Order? How is it that the IRA is considered an illegal organisation while the Masonic Order is not considered an illegal organisation?'

Oliver J. Flanagan (9 July 1943).

'The Blueshirts will be victorious in the Free State; the Blackshirts were victorious in Italy; the Hitlershirts were victorious in Germany.'

John Costello (2 February 1934).

'I had second thoughts about the Fine Gael Party. I know in the maniac ideas they have, they have lost control so much that they have decided they must get control of this country by hook or by crook. They have decided the best way is to appeal to the teenagers in this country. I have nothing in the world against the teenagers but on the other hand, it is a shocking situation, in 1965, that anybody with ordinary common sense in his head, if he has a head or any brains in it, should adopt the attitude of appealing to these screamers who go down after the Beatles, the Rolling Stones and the other idiots who masquerade as some kind of paragon for our people today. I am surprised that the hierarchy or the clergy of the country have not tried to call a halt to this before now.'

J.R. Leneghan (17 February 1965).

'There were no tomahawks and no daggers in our councils, only candles that burned low, trying to protect simple people from the burden of a rising cost of living and to ensure that resources would be mobilised to put roofs over their heads.'

James Dillon (11 November 1966).

'Most people in public life will state their acceptance of the teachings contained in the papal encyclicals. But two dangers exist. Firstly, such acceptance may amount merely to lip service and, secondly, these principles may be used as an excuse for inaction.'

Fine Gael, 'Just Society' (26 May 1964).

'Any other policy of opposition would amount to a cynical exploitation of short-term political opportunities for a political advantage which would inevitably prove to be equally short-lived. I will not play that game because it would not produce any real or lasting advantage for the Irish people.'

Alan Dukes, announcing his Tallaght Strategy (September 1987).

'Unlike FFers, they tend to blush when caught lying or on the take from big business.'

Gene Kerrigan, *Never Make a Promise You Can't Break: How to Succeed in Irish Politics* (2002).

'Alan Dukes treated his front-bench colleagues as a senior psychiatrist treats a group of psychotic patients.'

Barry Desmond, in his memoir, *Finally and in Conclusion* (2000).

'Fine Gael is choking on an overdose of the liberal agenda.'

Jim Mitchell (21 May 1994).

'I have the face and the vision and I intend to use one to implement the other.'

Enda Kenny (2 February 2001).

'There will be no spokesmen for lawn mowers and forage harvesters.'

Michael Noonan, on his new front bench (9 February 2001).

'Unless it changes course quickly, Fine Gael will lose the battle for voters' minds . . . because it has become considerably more conservative than the vast majority of those who want to vote for us.'

Mary Banotti (21 May 1994).

'I think Fine Gael should set up a sanitation department we have had to clean up so often after Fianna Fáil.'

Michael Noonan, in his keynote speech to the Fine Gael Ard Fheis (14 February 2002).

'This is the first time that the opposition has been voted out of office.'

Charlie McCreevy, describing Fine Gael's disastrous performance in the 2002 general election.

Garret FitzGerald

The son of the revolutionary who carried a professorial air, Garret FitzGerald was Fine Gael's most successful leader and, in many ways, its most unpredictable. He has fashioned his own reputation for posterity in newspaper columns, learned contributions and several long tomes, including the 330,000-word autobiography All in a Life. If anyone ever gets around to reading them, let us know.

'People would totter out pale from exhaustion in the end, completely unable to remember what they said in the first six hours of the meeting.'

Fergus Finlay, on Garret FitzGerald's cabinet meetings, *Snakes and Ladders* (1998).

'During the four years in government, I spent what must amount to several months shut up in the cabinet room.'

Gemma Hussey, *At the Cutting Edge: Cabinet Diaries 1982–87* (1990).

'That's all very well in practice but will it work in theory?'

Garret FitzGerald (attrib.), during a cabinet meeting, quoted in Frank Dunlop, *Yes Taoiseach: Irish Politics from Behind Closed Doors* (2004).

'He explained about 800 years of English oppression and after he had finished I thought I had been through the entire 800 years.'

Margaret Thatcher, *The Downing Street Years* (1995).

'A cold, Garret FitzGerald mission to explain persona is death at the polls. Explaining things is fine for Dublin 4, but a problem nationally.'

Eoghan Harris, quoted in Emily O'Reilly, *Candidate: The Truth Behind the Presidential Campaign* (1991).

'This is so partitionist a state that Northern Protestants would be bloody fools to join it.'

Garret FitzGerald (11 February 1978).

'What I want to do is to lead a crusade – a Republican crusade – to make this a genuine republic on the principles of Tone and Davis . . . If I was a Northern Protestant today, I can't see how I could aspire to getting involved in a state which is itself sectarian.'

Garret FitzGerald (27 September 1981).

'We are on the brink of a unique breakthrough in Irish politics, that is, the emergence of Fine Gael as the larger single party in the State. Should this assessment be correct, and should we require additional support in the Dáil, we are prepared to discuss with the Labour Party the formation of a strong alternative government.'

Garret FitzGerald (4 June 1981).

'It was my fault. I'm to blame, but he isn't absent-minded about anything to do with his work. He is very much on the ball.'

Joan FitzGerald, after Garret was photographed wearing odd shoes (13 November 1982).

'Garret FitzGerald ran his government like a university debating society and the cabinet meetings lasted for ever.'

Frank Dunlop, *Yes Taoiseach: Irish Politics from Behind Closed Doors* (2004).

'Garret the Good.'

John Healy, nickname first used by in his column, 'Backbencher', in the *The Irish Times*.

'He's always Garret the Good. Garret has a halo, and Haughey has horns.'

Maureen Haughey (23 November 1982).

'The UDR in its present form, in its composition and in its discipline and performance is a force that Nationalists must and do fear. There have been just too many people murdered by the UDR either on duty or off duty.'

Garret FitzGerald (19 May 1985).

'Ulster says "no" to its minority. Can we say "no" to our people whose marriages have failed?'

Garret FitzGerald (25 June 1986).

'There seemed to be two Fianna Fáil parties, Fianna Fáil in opposition and Fianna Fáil in government, and any resemblance between them has become totally coincidental, in fact not only coincidental but almost unfindable at this stage.'

Garret FitzGerald, quoted in Stephen Collins, *The Power Game: Fianna Fáil since Lemass* (2000).

Diplomatic Incidents and Foreign Affairs

Ireland had consuls and ambassadors before it had a state. Like leaving politics to politicians, leaving diplomacy to diplomats is always a bad idea. It is not clear who exactly decided that fashioning an independent foreign policy meant avoiding the great power games all around. But they got away with it.

'England is our most important external affair. As Minister for External Affairs.'
Desmond FitzGerald (1924). Quoted in Ronan Fanning, *Independent Ireland* (1983).

'Let me remind the House of the Council of Constance in 1415, when the King of England applied for admission and was told that he did not represent one of the ancient nations of Christendom, and could not be admitted. When he found himself in that position he said, "but I have another string to my bow, I am also King of Ireland, and in that capacity I claim the right of admission", and in that capacity they let him in.'

George Gavan Duffy, speaking on proposal to join League of Nations, Dáil Éireann (18 September 1922).

'Friends of India, your course is identical to ours. We in Ireland, comparatively small in numbers, close to the heart of Britain's imperial power, have never despaired. You, people of India, remote from her, a continent in yourselves, seventy times as numerous as we are, surely you will not despair.'

Eamon de Valera, address to friends of India in New York (28 February 1920).

'When self-government is attained by Ireland, a consummation it is hoped is at hand, it should promptly be admitted as a member of the League of Nations.'

US Senate resolution passed during debate on Treaty of Versailles (19 March 1920).

'If you write something down people will know what you are going to do, are warned and may be in a position to stop you. So always keep your policy under your hat.'

Eamon de Valera explaining to Seán MacEntee why he never wrote down his foreign policy, quoted in John Bowman, *De Valera and the Ulster Question* (1982).

'Let us be frank with ourselves. There is on all sides complaint, criticism and suspicion. People are complaining that the League is devoting its activity to matters of secondary or very minor importance, while the vital international problems of the day, problems that touch the very existence of our peoples, are being shelved or postponed.

People are saying the equality of the states does not apply in the things that matter, that the smaller states, whilst being given a voice have little real influence.'

Eamon de Valera, address as President of League of Nations, Geneva (1932).

'Even as a partitioned small nation, we shall go on and strive to play our part in the world, continuing unswervingly to work for the cause of true freedom and for peace and understanding between all nations.'

Eamon de Valera (13 November 1935).

'It is generally admitted that the state which is known as Abyssinia, or, as someone reminds me, Ethiopia, is not as advanced as others in modern civilisation. For instance, it has not the same armaments as civilised countries have; it does not know how to use poison gas; it does not know how to blow up towns and cities as effectively as civilised nations are able to do so.'

Tom Johnson (13 November 1935). Ireland offered its defence forces to defend Ethiopia from invasion if the other big powers would follow.

'In the old days when the Catholics of Ireland were in trouble, the people of Spain came to our aid. Spain calls on us today not for military aid but to recognise that General Franco's fight is a fight for Christianity. I now put it to the Taoiseach to tell us what he is going to do, and to give a clear indication that he is a Catholic leader of a Catholic country and that at last he will do what we have been asking him to do for years.'

Captain Patrick Giles (13 July 1938).

'Is our conception of a nation only that of a parish pump? Has it not gone beyond the threadbare howl for a republic for the thirty-two counties that the Minister for Industry and Commerce shouts now and then, but that he has no more notion of achieving than of reaching the moon?'

Paddy Belton, Dáil Éireann (19 February 1937).

'What are Russia, Italy, Germany and France arming for? The Olympic Games?'

Paddy Belton, Dáil Éireann (19 February 1937).

'The war in Spain is a war for the victory or defeat of communism and all it stands for, with its denial of Christian principles, individual liberty and democracy. I do not see how a country with our history, our beliefs, our traditions and our ideals, moral, religious and political, can fail to withdraw recognition from a government which stands for everything we abhor.'

William T. Cosgrave (27 November 1937).

'It is far better for Britain, far more advantageous for Britain, to have a free Ireland by its side than an Ireland that would be unfriendly because of liberties which Britain denied.'

Eamon de Valera (27 April 1938).

'If it should be that we are attacked, our people and our friends everywhere in the world will already have known of our determination to resist, and that to the utmost of our power. To such a situation we shall endeavour to bring the same spirit which has made our history a story of one of the most devoted struggles for liberty in the history of mankind.'

Eamon de Valera (1941).

'They've all gone mad out there.'
Fianna Fáil senator during World War II.

'The Germans and the Italians are not the people who murdered and robbed my people. It took your good English friends to do that and they continue to do that.'
Bob Briscoe TD, who is Jewish, on Irish neutrality during WWII, quoted in Eunan O'Halpin, *Fianna Fáil and Neutrality in Taking the Long View* (1996).

'[De Valera is] probably the most adroit politician in Europe and he honestly believes that all he does is for the good of the country. He has the qualities of martyr, fanatic and Machiavelli. No one can outwit him, frighten him or brandish him.'
David Gray, US Minister in Dublin, in a message to President Roosevelt (10 November 1940).

'[David Gray] had the temerity to make it plain to Irish Nationalists that they were no longer the darling Playboy of the Western World, and to point out that the audience were bored.'
John Maffey, British Representative in Dublin (25 February 1943). Quoted in Thomas Lyle Dwyer, *Irish Neutrality and the USA 1939–1947* (1977).

'We request that the Irish Government take appropriate steps for the recall of German and Japanese representatives in Ireland.'
David Gray, US Minister in Dublin, in a formal note presented to Taoiseach Eamon de Valera (21 February 1944).

'A few well-placed bombs on the Irish barracks at the Curragh

and in the Dublin area would be the most merciful way of
shutting off opposition.'

David Gray, US Minister in Ireland, to President Roosevelt
(20 May 1942).

'I tried hard before the United States entered the war to get
de Valera to abandon neutrality and join in. I told him he
would not get away with it . . . but de Valera did get away
with it . . . Howbeit, that powerless little cabbage garden
called Ireland wins in the teeth of all the mighty powers.'

George Bernard Shaw, *Irish Press* (31 March 1944).

'There is no reason why Éire should not continue in
association with Britain but not as a formal member of the
British Commonwealth . . . the External Relations Act was
full of inaccuracies and infirmities and the only thing to do
was to scrap it.'

Taoiseach John A. Costello (7 September 1948).

'Irish Republic tonight at midnight. Hilton Edwards piously
thanked God that England was free at last from 700 years of
Irish domination.'

Micheál MacLiammóir, diary (17 April 1949).

'It took us a long time to build up our own culture and now
we are having an influx of foreign ideas.'

Captain Patrick Giles (30 April 1946).

'The Republic was not and could not be neutral in the issue
between communism and democracy, usually described as
the struggle between East and West.'

Liam Cosgrave (7 July 1956).

'Oh my God.'

Irish civil servant when Jack Lynch accidentally announced fly-over arrangements with Britain at dinner in the National Press Club in Washington (8 November 1979). It precipitated a party revolt that led to his resignation as Taoiseach.

'Ireland is pretty small potatoes compared to other countries of Europe. No great issues burn up the wires between Dublin and Washington, the high cost of goods, their unavailability, the dreary urbanscapes, the constant strikes and the long, dank and damp winters combine to gnaw away at one's enthusiasm for being here.'

Robin Berrington, US Embassy Cultural Affairs Officer (25 December 1980).

'It's already done. It is a fait accompli. On June 18, the referendum was held and 65 per cent of the people favoured it; 11 per cent opposed it.'

William FitzGerald, US ambassador designate (3 June 1992) – before the Maastricht referendum was held.

'In a week in which Americans discovered that their Vice President couldn't spell potato, Irish Americans discovered that their new ambassador to Ireland (a) didn't know what month it was and (b) couldn't tell the difference between Loyalists, Unionists and Nationalists.'

Irish Voice (21 June 1992).

'Glengall Street.'

Derisory reference to Department of Foreign Affairs during 1994-7 Rainbow Coalition. Glengall Street is the address of the Ulster Unionist Party headquarters in Belfast.

'We dine for Ireland.'

In-joke of Department of Foreign Affairs staff to newcomers.

'I'll cut off your champagne allowance.'

Charles J. Haughey, threat to Department of Foreign Affairs officials, quoted in Eamonn Delaney, *The Accidental Diplomat* (1998).

'Haughey regarded the Department of Foreign Affairs as gin-swilling arrivistes, with affected manners of speech and behaviour in whom he had very little confidence.'

Frank Dunlop, *Yes Taoiseach: Irish Politics from Behind Closed Doors* (2004).

'Can we now hope that all the sophistry, ambivalence and self-deception that has oozed out of Iveagh House for some time now will cease and that the cold harsh reality will be accepted: that Ireland's interests are best defended by Irishmen and women and that all the appeasement, the platitudes and honeyed words mean nothing when the chips are down. At the Brussels Summit we have seen the Taoiseach's reputation and the current favour-currying type of Iveagh House diplomacy exposed for what it is. At the crunch, when Ireland's vital interests were at stake, they were hardly taken seriously.'

Charles J. Haughey (21 March 1984).

'The Turko-Grecian War was like waiting for a train in Mullingar.'

Stephen MacKenna, translator and journalist (1872-1934).

Gaffes

Politicians are supposed to be able to think on their feet. Sometimes, they prefer to do other things with their feet.

'The idea is well and good in theory, but tell me this, who is going to feed the gondolas?'

Legend told about almost every council in Ireland where a local councillor objects to a proposal to boost tourism by putting gondolas in the town's water feature.

'I smelt a rat; I see him forming in the air and darkening the sky; but I'll nip him in the bud.'

Sir Boyle Roche (attrib.), speech in Irish House of Commons (1743–1807).

'Mr Speaker, if we once permitted the villainous French masons to meddle with the buttresses and walls of our ancient constitution, they would never stop nor stay, sir, till they brought the foundation stones tumbling about the ears of the nation.

Here, perhaps, sirs, the murderous Marshellaw men would break in, cut us to mincemeat, and throw our bleeding heads upon that table, to stare us in the face.'

Sir Boyle Roche, speech on threatened French invasion (1796).

'Are we to live, like the birds in the bushes – from hand to mouth?'

Christopher Coppinger, nineteenth-century politician.

'One must be careful not to prejudge the past.'

William Whitelaw, Secretary of State for Northern Ireland (25 March 1972).

'There could be ten or twelve urban councils and six or seven county councils on that river system. Most of those could be doing their job, but there might be a few niggers in the woodpile who would destroy the whole purpose of the legislation.'

Austin Deasy, Dáil Éireann (18 October 1979).

'It reminds me of a story of two niggers discussing the sale of a mule.'

Patrick McGilligan (12 July 1932).

'We never fought in this country to have a foreign nigger getting £12 a ton more for his sugar than an Irish farmer.'

Dan Corry (8 February 1967).

'It's about time people in this town didn't have to worry about whether they are going to be burned to death before they wake up in the morning.'

SDLP assembly member Danny O'Connor (12 January 2001).

'Stick with the kebabs.'

Conor Lenihan TD, to socialist TD Joe Higgins (21 May 2005).

'Three-quarters of what the opposition says about us is lies and the other half is without any foundation in truth.'

Sir Boyle Roche (attrib.), quoted in Des MacHale, *The Book of Irish Bull* (1987).

'Next week is another day.'

Peadar Clohessy (29 June 1989).

'I answer in the affirmative with an emphatic "No!"'

Sir Boyle Roche (attrib.), quoted in Des MacHale, *The Book of Irish Bull* (1987).

'The only way of preventing what is past is to put a stop to it, before it happens.'

Sir Boyle Roche (attrib.), quoted in Des MacHale, *The Book of Irish Bull* (1987).

'A disorderly set of people whom no king can govern and no God can please.'

Comment made about Northern Protestants, quoted in Henry Boylan, *Theobald Wolfe Tone* (1981).

'My mother told me never to worry about sticks and bones.'

Bertie Ahern, Dáil Éireann (May 2006).

'Every prime minister needs a Willie.'

Margaret Thatcher, farewell dinner for William Whitelaw (1999).

'Unlike Deputy Johnson, who manages to be a doctrinaire in two directions as it suits him, I am not a doctrinaire even in one.'

Kevin O'Higgins (3 May 1923).

'Charlie McCreevy is looking at the whole system, to dehumanise it.'

Albert Reynolds (15 November 1992).

'I don't want to encourage alarmistic vibrations.'

Joe Jacob telling broadcaster Marian Finucane about iodine pills (September 2001).

'Mister Speaker, the country is in such a desperate state that little children, who can neither, walk nor talk, are running around the street cursing their maker.'

Sir Boyle Roche (attrib.). Quoted in Des MacHale, *The Book of Irish Bull* (1987).

'We are not prepared to stand idly by and be murdered in our beds.'

Revd Ian Paisley (1997).

'We have to have something that the dead can live with.'

Sinn Féin official (1 August 1994).

'The Women's Coalition wish to be all things to all men.'
Sammy Wilson, DUP spokesman (14 September 1998).

'John Bruton is a convicted politician . . . a politician of conviction, I mean.'
Nora Owen (31 January 2001)

'The man who would stoop so low as to write an anonymous letter, the least he might do is to sign his name to it.'
Sir Boyle Roche (attrib.), quoted in Des MacHale, *The Book of Irish Bull* (1987).

Charles J. Haughey

Political and journalistic careers were made by Ireland's most controversial leader. He clocked up so many miles in his mid-career exile between 1970 and 1979 that he proved indestructible afterwards, even in the face of his own arrogance, his disastrous personal finances and his capacity to allow his political strokes to spring back in his face. He has already inspired his own folklore, several books (including the masterful *The Boss* by Joe Jennings and Peter Murtagh) and a television series. Without envying his divisive qualities, his successors envy the high levels of support the Fianna Fáil Party commanded under his despotic reign. It is likely that in centuries to come historians will focus on his achievements. Whatever it was he had, it wasn't learned in TD school.

'Deep down, I'm a very shallow person.'
Charles J. Haughey (attrib.).

'They are all my people. Now I know I will be leader.'
Charles J. Haughey, to Geraldine Kennedy (1977)

'When time elapses and when the balance sheet is totted up, the pluses and minuses, when his legislative achievements are placed in the balance against other matters, I think that his record will stand the test of time.'

P.J. Mara (22 May 2002).

'Of all the politicians with whom I worked, it will be no surprise if I say now that, for all his faults, the best of these was Charlie Haughey. When the last five Taoisigh come to be judged by historians, Charles Haughey will stand head and shoulders over the others in the public memory and perhaps, in time, in public affection.'

Frank Dunlop, *Yes Taoiseach: Irish Politics from Behind Closed Doors* (2004).

'A bizarre happening, an unprecedented situation, a grotesque situation, an almost unbelievable mischance.'

Charles J. Haughey, speaking at a Dublin press conference on the resignation of Attorney General Patrick Connolly after Malcolm McArthur, a man wanted for murder, was found at his home on 16 August 1982.

'You've got to hand it to the man, you really have. He is grotesque, unbelievable, bizarre and unprecedented, GUBU.'

Conor Cruise O'Brien (24 August 1982).

'I have done the state some service, and they know it, no more of that.'

Charles J. Haughey, final address to the Dáil, in which he quoted from W.B. Yeats and *Othello*.

'Haughey's bravery in 1987 to face up to the fact that this country did not have to be a banana republic with debt that was higher than Ethiopia and unemployment that was among the highest in the world, that we could in fact turn it around.'

Bertie Ahern, on Charles J. Haughey.

'He did the state. Some service.'

Letter writer to *The Irish Times* (10 February 1999).

'What politics should be about is making the world a better place for those you serve.'

Charles J. Haughey (1982).

'That was a difficult time, I remember it well. They were tough times but I think that as a programme it was good for a younger generation to understand all the good things Charlie Haughey has done.'

Bertie Ahern, on Charles J. Haughey.

'That sort of smug, know-all commentator – I suppose if anything annoys me, that annoys me. I could instance a load of fuckers whose throat I'd cut, and push over the nearest cliff, but there's no percentage in that.'

Charles J. Haughey, in an interview with John Waters, *Hot Press* (29 November 1984).

'Charlie always had the uncomplicated belief that the greater good was served by him getting what he wanted.'

Terry Keane, describing her twenty-seven-year affair with Charles J. Haughey (14 May 1999).

'Papandreou, my hero.'

Comment made by Haughey at the Athens Summit in 1989, when he saw Greek premier Andreas Papandreou with his young wife, Dimitra Liani, an Olympic Airways hostess, quoted in Tim Ryan, *P.J. Mara* (1992).

'Haughey isn't happy to be running the country. He wants to own it.'

Frank Cluskey, leader of the Labour Party (attrib.).

'I like the company of poets. They take you away from the boring realities of life, if you like, and open up all sorts of exciting things, sometimes quite startling.'

Charles J. Haughey (31 December 1990).

'Shrewd, tough, ruthless and ambitious.'

Andrew Gilchrist, British Ambassador, on Charles J. Haughey when he was Minister for Finance (10 November 1969).

'He apes the ways of the English ascendancy.'

Andrew Gilchrist, British Ambassador, on Charles J. Haughey when he was Minister for Finance (10 November 1969).

'I think an accountant often makes a very bad Minister for Finance.'

Charles J. Haughey (15 July 1997).

'At this point Mr Haughey became quite vicious and told Mr Denvir that "he would not give up his cheque book and he had to live" and "that we were dealing with an adult and no banker would talk to him in this manner". Furthermore he stated that if any drastic action were taken by the bank he could be a "very troublesome adversary".'

Allied Irish Bank official in a memo (1 October 1976), published on 19 February 1999 at Moriarty Tribunal.

'This dream account, or dream relationship, turned into what I would describe as a banker's nightmare.'

Gerry Scanlan, of Allied Irish Banks giving evidence to Moriarty Tribunal (18 February 1999).

'Mr Haughey is quite irresponsible in money matters. He cannot be controlled on a running account. His affairs can only deteriorate further.'

J.J. McAuliffe, Allied Irish Banks General Manager, in an internal memo (15 January 1975), published on 16 February 1999 at the Moriarty Tribunal.

'It has been rumoured in discreet financial circles for years that Mr Haughey owed £1 million to a major bank and that the bank had held its hand because of his elevated position. This correspondent can confirm that sources close to Allied Irish Banks insist that he owed them around this sum last year.'

Des Crowley, *Evening Press* (28 January 1983).

'This statement is so outlandishly inaccurate that Allied Irish Banks feels bound, as a special matter to say so positively and authoritatively.'

AIB statement (31 January 1983). Haughey owed £1.4 million; someone settled £750,000 of it and the bank wrote off the rest.

Ben Dunne: 'Look, here's something for yourself.'

Charles J. Haughey: 'Thank you, big fella.'

Ben Dunne, at the McCracken Tribunal, describing how he gave three bank drafts worth £70,000 each to Charles J. Haughey in 1991 (22 April 1997).

'I now accept that I received the £1.3 million from Mr Ben Dunne and that he handed me £210,000 in Abbeville in November 1991.'

Charles J. Haughey, to the McCracken Tribunal (9 July 1997).

'My private finances were purely peripheral to my life. I left them to Mr Des Traynor to look after. I didn't have a lavish lifestyle. My work was my lifestyle and when I was in office I worked every day, all day. There was no room for any sort of an extravagant lifestyle.'

Charles J. Haughey (15 July 1997).

'Farcical, absurd, grossly unfair and iniquitous.'

Charles J. Haughey, starting his High Court challenge to Moriarty Tribunal investigation of his finances (25 March 1998).

'I asked myself what country was I living in. Was I living in Russia after the revolution?'

Maureen Haughey (25 March 1998).

'I do, yes. He should be convicted.'

Mary Harney, in an *Irish Independent* interview, when asked if Haughey should spend time in prison (27 May 2000). Her remarks caused the collapse of court proceedings against Haughey.

'They have a bust of me here.'

Charles J. Haughey, to officials at the Charvet shirt shop in Paris, where he had stopped to pick up a consignment of shirts, quoted in Stephen Collins, *The Power Game: Fianna Fáil since Lemass* (2000).

'The Bill seeks to provide an Irish solution to an Irish problem.'

Charles J. Haughey, proposing a Bill allowing contraceptives to be available on a doctor's prescription (28 February 1979).

'Davis had said, "A free people can afford to be generous. A struggling people cannot and should not be so." . . . I cannot accept this self-abasement, this suggestion that we in the Republic have something to be ashamed of because of Partition.'

Charles J. Haughey (28 September 1981).

'Eamon de Valera and his comrades had at all times to fight against the remnants of that colonial mentality that still linger on in Irish life. We can see emerging once more in modern Ireland that mentality we will not apologise to anyone for being what we are.'

Charles J. Haughey (11 October 1981).

'Deputy Haughey presents himself here, seeking to be invested in office as the seventh in this line, but he comes with a flawed pedigree. His motives can be judged ultimately only by God but we cannot ignore the fact that he differs from his predecessors in that these motives have been and are widely impugned, most notably but by no means exclusively, by people within his own party, people close to him who have observed his actions for many years and who have made their human, interim judgement on him. They and others, both in and out of public life, have attributed to him an overweening ambition which they do not see as a simple emanation of a desire to serve but rather as a wish to dominate, even to own the State.'

Garret FitzGerald (11 December 1979).

'This debate, essentially is about the evil spirit that controls one political party in this Republic, and it is about the way in which that spirit has begun to corrupt the entire political system in our country. This is a debate about greed for office, about disregard for truth and about contempt for political standards. It is a debate about the way in which a once-great party has been brought to its knees by the grasping acquisitiveness of its leader. It is ultimately a debate about the cancer that is eating away at our body politic – and the virus which has caused that cancer, An Taoiseach, Charles J. Haughey.'

Dick Spring, Labour Party Leader, opening a debate on Charles J. Haughey (31 October 1990).

'If I saw Mr Haughey buried at midnight at a crossroads, with a stake driven through his heart – politically speaking – I should continue to wear a clove of garlic round my neck, just in case.'

Conor Cruise O'Brien, *The Observer* (10 October 1982).

'It is my duty as Minister for Agriculture to inspect the drains of North Dublin.'

Charles J. Haughey, after falling off a horse while hunting with the North Dublin hunt, quoted in Eric Craigie, *History of the North Dublin Hunt*.

'Charles Haughey is head, shoulders and feet above everyone else in Fianna Fáil.'

Ned O'Keeffe (attrib.).

'Some of these Chinese leaders can go on until they are eighty or ninety, but I think that is a bit long really.'

Charles J. Haughey (he was joking, we think) (22 September 1991).

'It was like Alice on a night out with Franz Kafka in wonderland.'

P.J. Mara, on life with Charles J. Haughey, quoted in Tim Ryan, *P.J. Mara* (1992).

Haughey: 'If you have any respect for the office you should call me Taoiseach.'

Dick Walsh: 'It is because I have respect for the office that I call you Charles Haughey.'

Exchange at press conference.

'The arrogance, insensitivity and gross misjudgement he deployed yesterday proved once and for all [. . .] that Ireland deserves better . . . Taoiseach you must, today, consider your position. You must go, and go now.

Dick Spring (14 November 1991).

'Having a bill service is a feature of modern life.'

Charles J. Haughey (25 May 2001).

'There was a decision taken in Cabinet that the leaking of matters from Cabinet must be stopped. I, as Minister for

Justice, had a direct responsibility for doing that, I did that. I do feel that I was let down by the fact that people knew what I was doing.'

Seán Doherty, revelation on RTÉ programme *Nighthawks*, which brought down Charles J. Haughey (15 January 1992).

'I am tired, and the country is tired, of the hypocrites of virtue, ever ready with the instant moral judgement, the accusing finger.'

Charles J. Haughey (14 November 1991).

'The teapot.'

Reference to Haughey by girls in Fianna Fáil office, quoted in Tim Ryan, *P.J. Mara* (1992).

'I am confirming tonight that the Taoiseach, Mr Haughey, was fully aware in 1982 that two journalists' phones were being tapped and that he at no stage expressed a reservation about this action . . . As soon as the transcripts became available I took them personally to his office . . . I took the blame when Mr Haughey stated on RTÉ radio that he would "not have countenanced" such an action, and described it as an "abuse of power".'

Seán Doherty (21 January 1992).

'I wish to state categorically that I was not aware at the time of the tapping of these telephones and that I was not given and did not see any transcripts of the conversations.'

Charles J. Haughey (22 January 1992).

'They are only a crowd of gobshites.'

Charles J. Haughey, describing his ministerial colleagues, in conversation with unnamed backbencher (5 July 1989). Quoted in Stephen Collins, *The Power Game: Fianna Fáil since Lemass* (2000).

'I would like to thank him for bringing us into being and bringing us into government.'

Michael McDowell on Charles J. Haughey, Dáil Éireann (June 2006).

'He was witty. He was quick. He was determined. And he wanted you to be determined.'

Brendan Kennelly, funeral oration for Charles J. Haughey (2006).

'My mother used to say everyone hates Charlie Haughey except the people.'

Sean Haughey, funeral oration for Charles J. Haughey (2006)

I said at the time, I think Haughey is making a huge mistake, trying to get six or seven people together. Christ picked twelve apostles and one of them crucified him.'

Ben Dunne, at the McCracken Tribunal (2 April 1997)

'Deeply flawed but utterly compelling.'

Fintan O'Toole (2 February 2002).

Health

One quarter of the national budget goes into trying to provide a health service. No wonder it is such an unhealthy place for a politician. Surprisingly for such a big issue, it was scarcely considered worth a mention in the early days. The Department of Health was tagged on to local government until 1947 and then had Social Welfare attached to it. Outsourcing the building of hospitals to the Irish Hospitals Sweepstakes and the running of them to religious orders and charity trusts seemed like a masterstroke. No wonder politicians were surprised when it came back to bite them in 1948. Since then, the vested interests in health have proven some of the most resourceful in the business; three governments have fallen on health issues, and few people have been brave enough to try anything smelling of reform.

'More landmines than Angola.'

Brian Cowen (attrib.), on the Department of Health, reported by PR man Paul Allen during meeting with Harcourt Street Children's Hospital Support Group (4 February 1999).

'One day I was walking up to Bewley's for a coffee and a bun lunch and as usual I was accompanied by J.D. McCormack. I said to J.D. quite suddenly, "I've got to name this thing. We'll call it the Mother and Child Service; that should sell it. No one could oppose a scheme with a name like that."'

James Deeny, Chief Medical Officer of the Department of Health, in *To Cure and to Care: Memoirs of a Chief Medical Officer* (1989).

'There is a real danger that it will pauperise the people and prostitute the profession. Pregnancy certainly should not be raised or lowered to the status of a dangerous disease.'

Dr P. Moran, President of Irish Medical Association, opposing the Mother and Child Scheme to provide free medical care (7 July 1949).

'In relation to the birth of your child and the growth of that child up to the age of sixteen years, you will have no more doctor's bills to pay.'

Noel Browne, promoting Mother and Child Scheme on radio, quoted in Maev-Ann Wren, *Unhealthy State: Anatomy of a Sick Society* (2003).

'I could never understand why anybody should stand over a scheme which involved the old-age pensioner in Connemara and the agricultural labourer in Laois-Offaly paying for the rich lady in Foxrock when she was having her children.'

John A. Costello (13 May 1951).

'The health authorities seem to think that if a man's body is as twisted as a corkscrew, it does not matter because he is not going to die of it. A man can have a body shaped like an

S-hook, but, because he will not die of it, the medical profession do not take a serious view of it.'
Frank Sherwin (30 June 1960).

'Since the Famine, Ireland has controlled its population growth by three measures: celibacy, late marriage and emigration.'
Annual Report of the Medico-Social Research Board (8 May 1971).

'You'd swear we didn't have a health service at all.'
Fianna Fáil canvasser during general election (3 June 1989).

'A hospital trolley is merely a bed on wheels.'
Dr John O'Connell (3 June 1989).

'A two-tier system has been the position since the foundation of the state and this system, with its integrated mix of public and private care, has served the nation well.'
Rory O'Hanlon, Minister for Health 1987-9. Quoted in Maev-Ann Wren, *Unhealthy State: Anatomy of a Sick Society* (2003).

'The Minister is enshrining in our system a permanent separation, a fast lane for those who can afford and a slow lane for those who cannot.'
Richard Bruton, Dáil Éireann (18 May 1991).

'I hope my winning a seat will add colour and flavour to the proceedings, but that my professional expertise, psychiatry, will not be called on too often.'
Dr Moosajee Bhamjee (16 December 1992).

'The government really required the public system to be inferior. Why else, if it was first rate, would people pay for a private system?'

Brendan Howlin, Minister for Health 1994–7, quoted in Maev-Ann Wren, *Unhealthy State: Anatomy of a Sick Society* (2003).

'Spending has been quadrupled since 1992/1993. I don't think the Irish people are that much more ill in that period of time.'

Charlie McCreevy, quoted in Maev-Ann Wren, *Unhealthy State: Anatomy of a Sick Society* (2003).

'There are significant inequalities in the system at present.'

Government Health Strategy (2001).

'This is accountancy, not a health service.'

Dr David Lillis, commenting on the decision to reduce the number of beds in University College Hospital Galway (October 1998).

'If a superior system is demanded by the public, and there is much evidence to believe this is the case, than, as taxpayers, the financial implications of addressing the current health service deficits need to be accepted.'

Deloitte & Touche, in conjunction with the York Health Economics Consortium on behalf of the Department of Health and Children, 'Value for Money Audit of the Irish Health System' (2001).

'It is not a case of throwing money into a black hole.'

Micheál Martin, Minister for Health 2002–4. Quoted in Maev-Ann Wren, *Unhealthy State: Anatomy of a Sick Society* (2003).

'We want the elderly to be able to live out their retirement in dignity and security without having to worry about the State confiscating their savings.'
Mary Harney (November 1996).

'I know this seems controversial, but is it fair that people require the State to pick up the bill, and then they get the benefits when people die? I genuinely believe we need to do more to encourage families to care for their loved ones.'
Mary Harney (16 January 2004).

'Could her solicitors not, in seeking a test case from the hundreds of hepatitis C cases on their books, have selected a plaintiff in a better condition to sustain the stress of a High Court case? Was it in the interest of their client to attempt to run her case, not only in the High Court but also in the media and in the Dáil simultaneously?'
Michael Noonan, speaking in Dáil Éireann (16 October 1996). Members of hepatitis-C pressure group Positive Action, who were viewing from the public gallery subsequently walked out and Mr Noonan later apologised.

'We would not allow food to be produced in the kind of hygiene environment in which patients are treated, and that is not acceptable.'
Mary Harney, Minister for Health (2001).

'It wasn't a cut. It was constructive reallocation of resources. Now, which would you prefer – a hundred thousand being wasted by the other crowd or ninety thousand constructively spent by Fianna Fail.'

Brian Lenihan, speaking on RTÉ television in the aftermath of the 1987 election, when he was accused of implementing health cuts.

'The Health [Family Planning] (Amendment) Bill has serious implications for moral behaviour. Casual and promiscuous sexual behaviour is always morally wrong. It is also acknowledged to be a major factor in the spread of AIDS.'

Catholic hierarchy (17 July 1992).

John Hume

A man whose career started in a resistance movement has managed to poke at the point of least resistance down the decades, to the extent that he has helped foster a reputation verging on infallibility. Some harsh words have been thrown his way by Unionist and Republican opponents, by more radical party colleagues and by an occasional Dublin journalist with a little too much indignation stuck up their nostrils. Managing to keep an inoffensive manner in the face of all this would be the dream of every politician. They should check out John Hume's Nobel acceptance speech from 1999 for details of how to do it.

'[Nationalist] leadership has been the easy leadership of flags and slogans. Easy no doubt but irresponsible. It is the lack of positive contribution and the apparent lack of interest in the general welfare of Northern Ireland that has led many Protestants to believe that the Northern Catholic is politically irresponsible and therefore unfit to rule.'

John Hume, *The Irish Times* (18 May 1964).

'The plan stands clear. [It is] to develop the strongly Unionist Belfast-Coleraine-Portadown triangle and to cause a migration from west to east 'Ulster', redistributing and scattering the minority so the Unionist Party will not only maintain but strengthen its position.'

John Hume, protesting at a London meeting over a decision by Stormont to site a new university at Coleraine rather than Derry (30 June 1965). Quoted in Paul Routledge, *John Hume* (1998).

'I am not a law-breaker by nature but I am proud to stand here with 15,000 Derry people who have broken a law which is in disrepute. I invite Mr Craig to arrest the lot of us.'

John Hume (16 November 1968).

'The truth is that Ulster Unionists are not loyal to the Crown, but the half-crown.'

John Hume (21 August 1969).

'The Border is a sectarian border. To attempt to use force to break it down would lead not only to civil war but to a religious war. There are hostages in Derry and hostages in Belfast. We are the ones who would suffer.'

John Hume (9 December 1969).

'We have opted out of Northern Ireland for the last 50 years and we must involve ourselves now. Many people would not like to join the UDR because it was against their traditions but Catholics must move in to make it a neutral force and prevent it being taken over by the B Specials.'

John Hume (12 March 1970).

'Their impartial role has now clearly ended. We cannot continue to give our consent to a continuation of the present situation. If our demand is not met by Thursday next, we will withdraw immediately from parliament.'

John Hume, SDLP deputy leader, demanding an inquiry into shooting of Catholic civilians Seamus Cusack and Desmond Beattie by the British army in Derry (11 July 1971).

'Today we do not recognise the authority of the Stormont Parliament and we do not care twopence whether this is treason or not.'

John Hume, SDLP deputy leader, at a meeting of the alternative assembly for Northern Ireland in Dungannon (26 October 1971).

British army general: 'You are trespassing on government property.'

John Hume: 'You are trespassing on my country.'

Exchange at protest march on Magilligan Strand (March 1972).

'I'll sit here until there is shit flowing up Royal Avenue and then the people will realise what these people are about and then we'll see who wins.'

John Hume, during a Unionist strike against the power-sharing executive (28 May 1974).

'[Edward Carson once said] that Unionism's last fight would be between the forces of the right and the forces of the Crown. That's it all started now.'

John Hume, after the fall of Sunningdale (May 1974).

'An approach which seeks to exclude other traditions leads only to the grave, destruction, death and conflict. It may satisfy the bugles in the blood, it may satisfy the atavism in everyone, we may feel proud of it, but it will not succeed.'

John Hume (19 June 1975).

'A twister, a political Jesuit twister.'

Eileen Paisley (31 March 1976).

'Churchill's Dunkirk exhortation "The situation is serious but not desperate", is said to have evoked a somewhat bleary comment from an Irish listener. "Over here the situation is always desperate but never serious."'

John Hume, writing in US Journal *Foreign Affairs* (May 1980).

'It is a commentary on the politics of the North of Ireland – or the fact that there is a problem there – that never before has someone with either my religious or political persuasion stood in the House to represent the city of Derry.'

John Hume, in his maiden speech to the House of Commons (28 June 1983).

'Unionists talk always of the past. Their thoughts are encapsulated in that marvellous couplet: "To hell with the future and long live the past, May God in his mercy look down on Belfast."'

John Hume (26 November 1985).

'The Protestant boil had to be lanced. Mrs Thatcher is the right person in the right place in the right time and they are recognising that she will not be broken.'

John Hume (17 April 1986).

'If you took the word "No" out of the English language, most of the Unionists would be speechless.'
John Hume (6 March 1987).

'I sincerely hope that no one will fall into the trap that has been laid by retaliating, because the doctrine of an eye for an eye leaves everyone blind.'
John Hume (9 November 1987).

'The Unionists may forgive me for reminding them that they have always been a party of the nineties – the sixteen nineties!'
John Hume (5 November 1989).

'I am not asking you [the IRA] to disappear. I am asking you to lay down your arms and join the rest of us in facing up to this enormous task of healing divisions.'
John Hume (3 March 1992).

'Northern Ireland is not a natural political entity.'
John Hume (26 September 1992).

'I apologise to no one for talking to Mr Adams. If I fail to achieve the objective of bringing violence to an end, the only damage will be that I have failed, but not a single person extra will be supporting violence as a result. However if the talks succeed, then the entire atmosphere will be transformed.'
John Hume (30 April 1993).

'I don't give two balls of roasted snow what advice anybody gives me about those talks, because I will continue with them until they reach a positive conclusion.'
John Hume (18 September 1993).

'The only sign of a border left in a unified Europe are British military checkpoints on the Irish Border. What are they there for? To deal with people who want rid of the Border.'

John Hume (1 February 1994).

'My dream is to see Ireland regarded as an off-shore island both of the United States of America and the United States of Europe, and given special treatment by both because it has played a major role in both.'

John Hume (19 September 1994).

'In 1912 the Ulster Unionists defied the sovereign wish of Parliament to grant Home Rule. That taught them a lesson which they have never forgotten – that if one threatens a British government or British parliament and produces crowds on the streets from the Orange lodges, the British will back down.'

John Hume (26 November 1985).

'Consider the bitterness of the European conflict over the centuries, and the 35 million dead in 1945; yet fifty years later there is a European Union. But the Germans are still German and the French are still French. How did they do it? Exactly as I am trying to do here, by building institutions that respect their differences, gave no victory to either side, but allowed them to work together in their common interest, to spill their sweat not their blood, and thereby break down the barrier of centuries.'

John Hume (4 April 1996).

'Political leadership is like being a teacher. It's about changing

the language of others. I say it, and I go on saying it, until I hear the man in the pub saying it back to me.'
John Hume (21 December 1996).

'Now, after a quarter of a century of bloodshed, agony and destruction, they tell us that the armed struggle is stalemated and that neither they nor the British Army can win. What a tragedy for all of Ireland that they couldn't see this blindingly obvious truth twenty-five years ago, when we told them.'
John Hume, as leader of SDLP, rejecting an electoral pact with Sinn Féin in the absence of an IRA ceasefire (20 February 1997).

'My adult life . . . has been devoted to resolving the very serious crisis in the North. It is now at a very crucial stage and therefore I feel it is my duty to stay with my colleagues in the SDLP and to continue to devote all my energies towards achieving a new and agreed Ireland, based on a lasting settlement and a lasting peace.'
John Hume, declining Fianna Fáil's offer of nomination as their presidential candidate (9 September 1997).

'John Hume has throughout been the clearest and most consistent of Northern Ireland's political leaders in his work for a political solution . . . David Trimble showed great political courage when at a critical stage of the process, he advocated solutions which led to the peace agreement.'
Nobel Committee (16 October 1998).

'I always kept repeating myself – it's the old teacher in me – that I hope that, in the future, the symbol of our patriotism will be the spilling of our sweat and not the spilling of our blood.'

John Hume (16 October 1998).

'The European Union is the best example in the history of the world of conflict resolution and it is the duty of everyone, particularly those who live in areas of conflict, to study how it was done and to apply its principles to their own conflict resolution.'

John Hume (10 December 1998).

'Most profoundly of all, we owe this peace to the ordinary people of Ireland, particularly those in the North who have lived and suffered the reality of our conflict.'

John Hume (10 December 1998).

Immigration

People having to move away from their homeland in search of a better life: that's a challenge for any politician. Now where did we come across this one before?

'If the Three Wise Men arrived here tonight, the likelihood is they would be deported.'

Proinsias De Rossa (18 December 1997).

'In the 1980s, tens of thousands of our people were illegal in the United States. We had politicians crossing the Atlantic every month begging for them to be made legal. The very least we can do is to afford the same to people who have sought refuge here.'

Joe Higgins (7 February 1998).

'The Minister is fearful that they will become involved in Irish life and, in effect, stop being statistics and start being human beings. It is not easy to deport people when they have been someone's neighbour, friend or work colleague.'

Liz McManus TD (December 1998).

Insults

With politicians comes parliamentary privilege. It means that they can say anything about you or me and not get sued for defamation. But you can't say anything about them in return. A good deal, but guess who drew up the rules?

'Ní thrácht ar an mhinisteir Gallda, / Ní ar a chreideamh gan bheann, gan bhrí, / Mar níl mar bhuan-chloch di theampuill, / Ach magairle Annraoí.' ('Don't speak of the alien minister, / Nor of his church without meaning or faith, / For the foundation stone of his temple / Is the bollocks of Henry the Eighth.')

Quoted and translated in Brendan Behan, *Borstal Boy* (1958).

'The Irish are a fair people – they never speak well of one another.'

James Boswell, *Life of Johnson* (1775).

'The hired traducer of his country – the excommunicated of his fellow-citizens – the regal rebel – the unpunished ruffian – the bigoted agitator. In the city a firebrand – in the court a liar – in the streets a bully – in the field a coward. And so obnoxious is he to the very party he wishes to espouse, that he is only supportable by doing those dirty acts the less vile refuse to execute.'

Henry Grattan, on John Giffard, an eighteenth-century official nicknamed 'the dog in office.'

'Under the Constitution of the Irish Free State you have no right to call any girl a shoneen because she walks into a dance at the vice-regal lodge.'

Mary MacSwiney (21 December 1921).

'I was advocating women's suffrage in Ireland when Count Plunkett was hanging out flags to receive the King of England.'

Arthur Griffith (2 March 1922).

'We are all acquainted with the phrase, 'There's a bee in his bonnet.' It strikes me in the case of Deputy Figgis he has a fish in his bonnet, and judging by the number of times that this matter has been brought up here by him it is not a very fresh fish at the moment.'

D.J. Gorey (6 December 1923).

'Nationalists to the right. Cromwellians and neo-Cromwellians, shoneen-Cromwellians and imitation Cromwellians to the left, the issue between something which is active, something which is real, something which means to be productive, and something which boasts of its impotence.'

H.V. Flinn (26 April 1928).

'I suppose the Minister for Local Government and Public Health may in his own way think he is the Cassius of the

Government of this House. I do not know what character Deputy Davis might take unless he might find it in Dickens.'

P.J. Ruttledge (17 June 1931).

'Is the Minister to be allowed to use the word idiotic in reference to a deputy? Is that a parliamentary remark?'

Gerry Boland (27 April 1928).

D.J. Gorey: 'That is a bloody lie.'

Leas-Cheann Comhairle Patrick Hogan: 'The Deputy has stated in my hearing that a statement of Deputy Corry is a lie. He used an adjective connected with it which I will not repeat. That statement must be withdrawn.'

D.J. Gorey: 'I withdraw it, and will say the statement is untrue.'

Leas-Cheann Comhairle Patrick Hogan: 'That statement cannot be allowed to pass either.'

D.J. Gorey: 'How am I to describe it then?'

Leas-Cheann Comhairle Patrick Hogan: 'It is not my function to tell the Deputy how to describe it.'

D.J. Gorey: 'It is inaccurate then.'

J.J. Byrne: 'Grossly inaccurate.'

Mr Corry: 'No one takes notice of the bull that gets out of its stall.'

D.J. Gorey: 'We are getting chastised by the baboon.'

Leas-Cheann Comhairle Patrick Hogan: 'I cannot allow this to continue. No Deputy can be allowed to call another

Deputy names. That statement must be withdrawn.'

D.J. Gorey: 'Deputy Corry must withdraw his statement about me.'

Leas-Cheann Comhairle Patrick Hogan: 'I have not heard that statement. If the Deputy made a statement which is not in accordance with Parliamentary procedure he will have to withdraw it.'

J.J. Byrne: 'He compared the Deputy to a bull which had escaped from a stall.'

Leas-Cheann Comhairle Patrick Hogan: 'That statement will have to be withdrawn also.'

J.J. Byrne: 'Certainly both sides must get fair play.'

D.J. Gorey: 'Very well, I withdraw.'

Dáil debate on Finance Bill (22 April 1932).

'I think Hitler and Mussolini would be ashamed to acknowledge the Deputies opposite as Fascists.'

Seán Lemass (8 February 1934).

'Lung power is the only power the Deputy possesses.'

H.V. Flinn (1 January 1934).

'Though the Inter-Party Government had a full majority of this House in 1956, the moment trouble came they ran and they ran like rats.'

Martin Corry (9 November 1965).

'I had a hope that after four or five general elections we would succeed in getting a number of new faces on the benches opposite and that there would be a different mentality there. The new ones appear to be worse than the old ones. We must only keep on taking them to the country until we get rid of the whole tribe.'

Martin Corry (6 July 1938).

'The Ministers and the Government are going on a picnic, but have they got a tin-opener?'

Michael Noonan, Fine Gael leader, in run up to general election (2002).

'Liam Lawlor is an exocet missile without a guidance system.'

Charles J. Haughey, quoted in Frank Dunlop, *Yes Taoiseach: Irish Politics from Behind Closed Doors* (2004).

'I was a witness of two murders. They took Noel Lemass into the mountains and bumped him off, riddled him with bullets. They crippled me and now say I have a pension. Deputy MacEoin has three pensions.'

Frank Sherwin (10 July 1963).

'Our ancestors cut a civilisation out of the bogs and meadows of this country while Mr Haughey's ancestors were wearing pig-skins and living in caves.'

Revd Ian Paisley, speech in Omagh (1981). Quoted in Ed Maloney and Andy Pollak, *Paisley* (1986).

'Brian Lenihan should be hauled in here and hung, drawn and quartered.'

Jim Mitchell (25 October 1990).

'Get back across the Shannon from whence you came. You come not in friendship but in guile.'

Mary O'Rourke speaking to Padraig Flynn (26 October 1990).

'It is time somebody stood up to him and told him he is not in the Congo now.'

Gus Healy, Fianna Fáil candidate, on Conor Cruise O'Brien, during a 1977 general election rally in Cork. An *Irish Times* poll during the campaign showed that Conor Cruise O'Brien and Charles J. Haughey were the two people that people would most dislike to see becoming Taoiseach. Quoted in T. Ryle Dwyer *Nice Fellow: A Biography of Jack Lynch* (2001).

'I kissed him, wasn't that good.'

Mary O'Rourke on losing her seat to running mate Donie Cassidy in the 2002 election (19 May 2002).

'Like a chimney sweep, rising laboriously through dirt and calling attention from the roof to his surprising elevation.'

John Philpot Curran, on Black Jack FitzGibbon, a determined social climber in the legal and political circles of the 1790s. He became attorney-general in 1784, lord chancellor between 1789-1802 and was created the earl of Clare in 1795.

'Mr Speaker, as the honourable gentleman has withdrawn what he has said about me, I withdraw what I was going to say I about him!'

Richard Baron Dowse, quoted in Timothy Healy, *Letters and Leaders of My Day* (1928).

'I think that there is no better exponent of codology in this

House than the leader of the Labour Party. He is the champion blatherskite of Ireland.'
Frank Aiken (10 December 1937).

'I am not acquainted with the web sites that Deputy Gormley stares at in the early hours of the morning, but one of them, www.indymedia.ie, has in the past produced interesting footage. On this occasion, it produced footage from outside of the Progressive Democrats party offices being ransacked by a group of Deputy Gormley's type of people. The anoraked group which descended on my party's offices would be the Deputy's friends.'
Michael McDowell, on Green Party deputy John Gormley.

'He's on the border-line of genius; but he never trespasses.'
Maurice Healy, *The Old Munster Circuit: A Book of Memories and Traditions* (1939).

'If what I say annoys Harold Wilson, it is because of his self-importance.'
Bernadette Devlin, *Evening Standard* (July 1969).

'He is the evil of two lessers.'
Michael McDowell describing Gay Mitchell.

'I do not mean to offend the Minister. I sometimes regret that so much of the bitterness has gone out of public life here because occasionally I find it hard to speak as I really think for fear of hurting someone on the far side for whom I have a genuine regard.'
John Kelly, quoted in John Fanagan (ed.), *Belling the Cats: Selected Speeches and Articles of John Kelly* (1992).

'I do not think that you are right in calling the President a Dago. He is no more a Dago than Deputy Nugget. A Dago is a Citizen of San Diego, and one who would certainly think it an impertinence if you called him an Irishman or held him responsible for the present mess. He is more Irish perhaps than any of us, seeing that he looks like something uncoiled from the Book of Kells.'

Oliver St John Gogarty, *As I Was Going Down Sackville Street* (1937).

'If anyone is justly described as an old fool, you may rest assured that he was also a young fool.'

John Pentland Mahaffy, quoted in W.B. Stanford and R.B. McDowell, *Mahaffy: A Biography of an Anglo-Irishman* (1971).

'A Ceausescu-era Olympic project.'

Michael McDowell, on the Abbotstown project (April 2002).

'Purple Turtle. First he turns purple, then he turns turtle.'

Revd Ian Paisley, on David Trimble (29 April 2003).

'Party colleagues would insist he was a fun guy to be with who liked nothing better than to bare his soul and let it all hang out. The naked truth is that he is as funny as vomit.'

Máirtin Ó Muilleóir, on Sammy Wilson, in *Belfast's Dome of Delight, City Hall Politics 1981–2000* (1999).

'I was enraged when I saw that strange character from Dublin coming again to see us. Somebody told me the other day that the reason his lips were so thick was that when his mother was bringing him up, he was a very disobedient boy. So she used to put glue on his lips and put him to the floor and keep him there, and that has been recorded in his physical make-up. What right has a foreign minister from Dublin to have a say in our affairs, our internal affairs? None whatsoever. Yes, away with him. If he wants to use his lips to better effect, he should do it somewhere else and do it with people of similar physical looks.'

Revd Ian Paisley (29 April 2003).

'He called me Ceausescu, but I didn't jump up looking for an apology.'

Bertie Ahern, commenting after McDowell compared Richard Bruton with Dr Goebbels.

'It is very difficult to remain in government if the leader of one party in effect charges the leader of the other party in the same government with perjury. We don't want to be in government for the sake of sitting at a desk.'

Desmond O'Malley (3 November 1992).

'That dirtbird down there will not get away with the allegations he made against me.'

Frank Sherwin (10 July 1963).

'I shall be asking a question about that dirtbird over there when you are finished.'

Frank Sherwin (18 July 1963).

'The Taoiseach could have been helpful on the ashes front as I have noticed he wears them himself once a year.

It may not be that painful. As he wears only clothes by Louis Copeland these days, I do not think he could help with the sackcloth.'

Joe Higgins (15 December 2004).

'I have the misfortune to be slightly deaf, and unfortunately Deputy Corry's voice strikes a deaf chord in my ears, and therefore I cannot answer the Deputy as I would wish, in a friendly manner.'

Major Cooper (19 April 1928).

'Dishonest, a coward and disrespectful to the people.'

Dr Edward T. Dwyer, Bishop of Limerick, on John Redmond, letter to the *Freeman's Journal* (14 July 1890).

'The head of the Government has been shown to be unsound in his judgement, treacherous in his relationships, vacillating in his decisions, incompetent in the management of his party and his Government.'

Charles J. Haughey (20 February 1986).

'He would come out with a fork if it started raining soup.'

John Donnellan, Fine Gael TD, on Alan Dukes (5 August 1989).

'He is a liar, a cheat, a hypocrite, a knave, a thief, a loathsome reptile which needs to be scotched.'

Revd Ian Paisley, on David Trimble (October 1998).

'It would take that motley bunch five years to agree on the time of the day.'

Noel Ahern (22 May 2002).

'A twit.'

Martin McGuinness, on David Trimble (11 March 2002).

'I wish the Minister well, and I hope his health improves, but his fig leaf is getting bigger and bigger because he has so many things to cover with it.'

Nora Owen, former Fine Gael Deputy Leader (7 July 2001).

'The PDs are lapdogs, not watchdogs of this government.'

John Gormley of the Green Party (3 March 2002).

'Come out from your Mercedes. You've been in it too long.'

Michael Noonan, speaking in Limerick, sending a message to Bertie Ahern (5 May 2002).

'You're like a cock who crows when the sun rises, after a while he thinks he is responsible for the sunrise.'

Michael Noonan, to Bertie Ahern (14 May 2002).

'Micheál Martin is a waste of space.'

Michael Noonan (14 May 2002).

IRA

Old revolutionaries don't grow old, not in Ireland anyway. They just split, and split and split. The original IRA became the Irish army, the second IRA merged into that army, the third, fourth and fifth evolved into various left-wing political parties. And the war carried on, with few victories, lots of draws and a mounting casualty list.

'I always carry gelignite; dynamite isn't safe.'
Brendan Behan (attrib.).

'The problem of partition cannot be solved by force . . . To allow any military body not subject to Dáil Éireann to be enrolled, organised and equipped is to pave the way to anarchy and ruin.'
Eamon de Valera (6 January 1957).

'[It] is a logical outcome of an obsession in recent years with parliamentary politics, with the consequent undermining of the basic military role of the Irish

Republican Army. The failure to provide the maximum defence possible of our people in Belfast is ample evidence of this neglect.'

IRA Provisional Army Council statement, signalling the birth of the Provisional IRA in protest at an 'Official' IRA convention which recognised the governments of London, Dublin and Belfast (28 December 1969).

'I Ran Away.'

Taunt used against IRA members after an assault on the Nationalist community. The IRA had seven guns with which to defend West Belfast and the hostage communities of Ardoyne and Turf Lodge (23 August 1969).

'When their answer to the just demand of the people are the lock-out, strike-breaking, evictions, coercions, the prison cell, intimidation or the gallows, then our duty is to reply in the language that brings these vultures to their senses most effectively, the language of the bomb and the bullet.'

Cathal Goulding, Chief of Staff of Official IRA, at a graveside oration in Cork (9 July 1971).

'The people of Derry are up now off their bended knees. For Christ's sake stay up. [People] should not shout "up the IRA", they should join the IRA.'

Maire Drumm (11 July 1971).

'The battle of the British Army hasn't been won, the losses of the IRA have been very slight . . . somewhat in the region of thirty men [two killed, the rest interned]. This is only a pinprick of the strength here.'

Joe Cahill, IRA Chief of Staff (13 August 1971).

'I don't think one can speak of defeating the IRA, of eliminating them completely, but it is the design of the security forces to reduce their level of violence to something like an acceptable level.'

Reginald Maudling, British Home Secretary (15 December 1971).

'The IRA truce had shown that they had a disciplined, tightly knit organisation.'

Harold Wilson (13 March 1972).

'If we become hesitant, the fight of this generation is lost. Concessions be damned. We want freedom.'

Seán Mac Stíofáin (2 April 1972).

'The overwhelming desire of all the people of the North is for an end to military action by all sides.'

Official IRA, announcing its ceasefire (29 May 1972).

'The IRA will suspend offensive operations as and from midnight on Monday, 26 June 1972, providing that a public reciprocal response is forthcoming from the armed forces of the British Crown.'

Provisional IRA (22 June 1972).

'1.   A public declaration by the British Government that it is the right of all the people of Ireland acting as a unit to decide the future of Ireland.

2.   A declaration of intent to withdraw British forces from Irish soil by 1 January 1975.

3.   A general amnesty.'

Provisional IRA conditions at a secret meeting (7 July 1972).

'Jesus, we have it!'

Seán Mac Stíofáin, IRA leader, to his comrades, in a break during a meeting of IRA and British ministers in London (7 July 1972). Quoted in Gerry Adams, *Before the Dawn* (1996).

'The truce between the Irish Republican Army and the British occupation forces was broken without warning by British forces at approximately 5.00 p.m. today at Lenadoon Estate, Belfast. Accordingly, all IRA units have been instructed to resume offensive action.'

Provisional IRA (8 July 1972).

'If Mr Whitelaw thinks that army behaviour will lead to our rejection of the Provisional IRA, he has grossly miscalculated. Military excesses create the need for a Provisional IRA.'

Paddy Devlin, SDLP chief whip, after his Andersonstown home was fired on by the British army (20 July 1972).

'She'll get a boot up the transom and be told to get out of our waters fast.'

Patrick Donegan, Minister for Defence, on the proposed action against the Cypriot coaster, *Claudia*, apprehended off Helvick Head with arms for the IRA (29 March 1973).

'The national leadership of the IRA did not order that attack. To the contrary, we condemn it. An attack like the one in Birmingham is murder.'

Dáithi Ó Conaill (11 December 1974).

'Today, we were unlucky, but remember we only have to be lucky once – you will have to be lucky always.'

P. O'Neill, statement after the attempted assassination of Margaret Thatcher (12 October 1984).

'Tiocfaidh ár lá.' ('Our day will come.')

Patrick Magee, IRA member, speaking after he was convicted of the Brighton bombing (11 June 1986).

'There haven't been any attacks by the IRA on Protestants.'

Gerry Adams (20 September 1986).

'In no way can, or will, the Provisional IRA ever be defeated militarily.'

General Sir James Glover, as former Head of Intelligence and Commander of British troops in Northern Ireland, speaking on the BBC's *Panorama* programme (29 February 1988).

'British Army bomb-disposal squads who attempt to defuse car bombs early and before areas are properly evacuated will be responsible for endangering civilian lives.'

IRA statement (1988).

'I have always believed we had a legitimate right to take up arms and defend our country and ourselves against the British occupation.'

Mairéad Farrell, IRA member killed by the SAS in Gibraltar in 1988.

'Recognising the potential of the current situation and in order to enhance the democratic peace process, the leadership of Óglaigh na hÉireann have decided that as of midnight, Wednesday August 31, there will be a complete cessation of military operations. All our units have been instructed accordingly.'

P. O'Neill (31 August 1994).

'You have to be cleverer than the IRA in intelligence, cleverer in action and cleverer politically. And to be perfectly blunt, we have failed in all three.'

Edward Heath (12 June 1993).

'It must be understood that there will never be any bargaining with those who in this democracy are being forced in arguments with bombs and bullets and the threat of violence.'

Patrick Mayhew, Secretary of State for Northern Ireland (25 October 1993).

'If the implication of [these] remarks is that we should sit down and talk with Mr Adams and the Provisional IRA, I would only say that would turn my stomach and those of most honourable members. We will not do it.'

John Major (1 November 1993).

'They haven't gone away, you know.'

Gerry Adams (13 August 1995).

'The IRA is committed to ending British rule in Northern Ireland. It is the root cause of divisions and conflict in our country. We want a permanent peace and therefore we are prepared to enhance the search for a democratic peace settlement through real and inclusive negotiations.'

P. O'Neill (20 July 1997).

'The British Government acted in bad faith, with Mr Major and the Unionist leaders squandering this unprecedented opportunity to resolve the conflict.'

The IRA, announcing the end of its seventeen-month ceasefire with the bomb blast at Canary Wharf in London (9 February 1996).

'We sued for peace. The British wanted war. If that's what they want we will give them another twenty-five years of war.'

P. O'Neill (1 March 1996).

'You don't have to all of a sudden start trusting people. You just have to show up, start, go to work . . . reach an agreement in good faith.'

Bill Clinton, message to the IRA (15 March 1996).

'The logical outcome is a new Stormont and the copper-fastening of partition. The only way forward [is] the armed struggle.'

Continuity IRA statement (2 September 1997).

'This phase of negotiations may fall apart, it may not succeed. And whenever that does happen, then we simply go back to what we know best.'

Francie Molloy, addressing republicans in South Armagh (15 November 1997).

'Don't kick the dog to see if it is still sleeping.'

Gerry Adams (30 September 1998).

Irish Americans

We never quite figured out how an island of 5.6 million people spawned 44 million more Irish on the other side of the Atlantic. The emergence of political leaders who promoted their Irish identity added a very peculiar dimension to transatlantic relationships. Bismarck famously bemoaned the shared language between England and the USA; in a peculiar way, so did England when things hotted up in Ireland.

'When St Patrick banished the snakes from Ireland they all came up on the other side of the Atlantic as Irish American politicians.'

James Larkin (attrib.).

'[Ireland's] sons and daughters are scattered throughout the world and they give this small island a family of millions upon millions . . . in a sense, all of them who visit Ireland come home.'

John F. Kennedy, US President, arriving at Dublin airport for a three-day visit to Ireland (27 June 1963).

'We welcome you as the representative of that great country in which our people sought refuge when driven by the tyrant's laws from their motherland, sought refuge and found themselves and their dependents a home in which they prospered, won renown and gave distinguished service in return.'

Eamon de Valera (27 June 1963).

'If this nation had achieved its present political and economic stature a century or so ago, my great-grandfather might never have left New Ross, and I might, if fortunate, be sitting down there with you. Of course, if your own President [Eamon de Valera] had never left Brooklyn, he might be standing up here instead of me.'

John F. Kennedy, address to the Oireachtas (28 June 1963).

'I think politics are hard in our country, but in Ireland where you have to run against somebody who is Irish all the time, it must be impossible.'

President Richard Nixon speaking at Dublin Castle during his three-day visit to Ireland (5 October 1970).

'Northern Ireland is becoming Britain's Vietnam . . . The Government of Ulster rules by bayonet and bloodshed. If only the cruel and constant irritation of the British military presence is withdrawn, Ireland can be whole again.'

Edward Kennedy (20 October 1971).

'It's tragic that so much is being done in the name of God, and it's the same God.'

Ronald Reagan (20 October 1979).

'Today, the British troops in Ulster have become an army of occupation. Stormont is now defunct in all but name and it is time for Britain to deliver the coup de grâce. The goal of reunification is now too close for Ireland to turn back.'

Edward Kennedy (28 February 1972).

'Once you've had a glass of Guinness with a man in Ireland, as I have with Brian Lenihan, why, you're friends.'

George Bush Senior (16 March 1990).

'Ireland's most precious gift to the world has been the Irish. No nation has benefited more from the talent of the Irish than the United States. Today over 44 million Irish-Americans reinforce the natural bond of friendship between our nations.'

President George W. Bush, St Patrick's Day Message (2001).

Irish Language

The revival of the Irish language was a key political goal of the 1920s and the major issue for at least one election in the 1960s, but, apart from that, politicians seem to allow it to hang on in the background out of harm's way. Despite the meddling of the politicians, the language hung on resiliently as a vibrant literary language, without becoming the language of business or everyday tongue for more than about 80,000 people. The Welsh, Icelanders and Israelis managed to use the lessons of Ireland in staging language revivals of their own.

'One demanded merrily why [Shane] O'Neill would not frame himself to speak English? What, quoth the other in a rage, thinkest thou that it standeth with O'Neill his honor to writhe his mouthe in clattering English?'

Richard Stanihurst, quoted in Holinshed, *Chronicles* (1587).

'Shortly before 1880 a Board of Education, which was called the Intermediate Board, was set up. That Board would have had no place for Irish if my friend and neighbour, the

O'Conor Don, had not obtained a place for the language when the bill was going through the English Parliament. The Board was permitted to examine students in Latin, Greek, and French, 'and in Celtic,' said the O'Conor Don, who was an MP at the time. "All right," they said, fed up with the whole business, "all right, in Celtic too." 'Celtic' was a nice respectable word that wouldn't have frightened any one. If he had said 'Irish', I doubt if he would have succeeded. But the only form of Celtic in Ireland is Irish.'

Douglas Hyde, *Mise an Conradh* (1931).

'His [Douglas Hyde's] volubility was as extreme as a peasant's come to ask for a reduction in rent. It was interrupted, however, by Edward [Martyn] calling on him to speak in Irish, and then a torrent of dark, muddied stuff flowed from him, much like the porter which used to come up from Carnacun to be drunk by the peasants on Midsummer nights when a bonfire was lighted. It seemed to me a language suitable for the celebration of an antique Celtic rite, but too remote for modern use. It had never been spoken by ladies in silken gowns with fans in their hands.'

George Moore, *Confessions of a Young Man* (1886).

'Di gcaillfi an Ghaeilge chaillfi tíre.' ('If Irish were to be lost, Ireland would perish.')

Padraig Pearse, *An Barr Buadh* (4 May 1916).

'I am sufficiently utilitarian not to regret its [the Irish language's] gradual abandonment. A diversity of tongues is no benefit; it was first imposed upon mankind as a curse, at the building of Babel. It would be of great advantage to mankind if all the inhabitants of the Earth spoke the same language.

Therefore though the Irish language is connected with many recollections that twine around the hearts of Irishmen, yet the superior utility of the English tongue, as the medium of all modern communication, is so great that I can witness without a sigh the gradual disuse of Irish.'

Daniel O'Connell (attrib.), quoted in Daunt O'Neill, *Personal Recollections of the late Daniel O'Connell, MP* (1848).

'My ambition had always been to use the language as a neutral field upon which all Irishmen could meet . . . So long as we remained non-political, there was no end to what we could do.'

Douglas Hyde, addressing the Ard Fheis, Dundalk (29 July 1915).

'If I were told tomorrow, "You can have a united Ireland if you give up your idea of restoring the national language to be the spoken language of the majority of the people", I would for myself say no.'

Eamon de Valera (7 February 1939).

'A people without a language of its own is only half a nation. A nation should guard its language – 'tis a surer barrier, and more important frontier, than fortress or river.'

Thomas Davis, *The Nation* (1 April 1843).

'In order-to de-Anglicise ourselves, we must at once arrest the day of the language. We must bring pressure upon our politicians not to snuff it out by their racist discourage lent merely because they do not happen themselves to understand it. We must arouse some spark of patriotic inspiration among the peasantry who still use the language, and put an end to the shameful state of feeling – a thousand-tongued reproach to our leaders and statesmen – which makes young men and women blush and hang their heads when overheard speaking their own language.'

Douglas Hyde, 'On the Necessity for De-Anglicising Ireland' (1892).

'To lose your native tongue, and learn that of an alien, is the worst badge of conquest – it is the chain on the soul. To have lost entirely the national language is death; the fetter has worn through.'

Thomas Davis, *Our National Language* (1914).

'To part with it would be to abandon a great part of ourselves, to lose the key of our past, to cut away the roots from the tree. With the language gone we could never aspire again to being more than half a nation.'

Eamon de Valera, in a radio broadcast (17 March 1943).

'The revivalists do not seek merely to revive a language, which task would be an objective one, susceptible of scientific planning and accomplishment. They seek to propagate the thesis that to be "Irish" (through and through) one must be a very low-grade peasant, with peasant concepts of virtue, jollity, wealth, success, and "art". To be a Gael, one has to change oneself, clothes, brogue and all, into the simulacrum of a western farm labourer.'

Flann O'Brien (Myles na gCopaleen), *The Best of Myles: A Selection from 'Cruiskeen Lawn'* (1968).

'Predetermined futility.'

The Times, on the teaching of Irish in schools (1893).

'More people speak Chinese to each other in Northern Ireland than speak Irish.'

John Taylor (19 August 1997).

'Loyalist leaders who express hostility to the Irish language are actually denying their own past. Not only is this past evident in many of their names (for example McCusker and Maginnis), it is obvious also in the fact that at the time of the Siege of Derry most of the population spoke Irish.'

Gerry Adams, *The Politics of Irish Freedom* (1986).

'You might as well be putting wooden legs on hens as trying to restore Irish through the school system.'

Eoin MacNeill, Minister for Education (1924). Quoted in J.J. Lee, *Ireland 1912–1985: Politics and Society* (1989).

'All the schooling was in English. There wasn't a syllable of Irish. It was against the law, and you would be beat if you used it. But the people had the Irish, and good Irish too, and they spoke it amongst themselves. Now the world has changed round, and you are paid to learn it and few people have it – it's a queer state of affairs.

Eric Cross, *The Tailor and Ansty* (1942).

Manus: 'What's 'incorrect' about the place-names we have here?'

Owen: 'Nothing at all. They're just going to be standardised.'

Manus: 'You mean changed into English?'

Owen: 'Where there's ambiguity, they'll be Anglicised.'

Brian Friel, *Translations: A Play* (1981).

'The money spent in attempting to turn this nation into a race of bilingualists ignorant and gullible in two languages, would have given Dublin spacious streets and boulevards and restored it to the place it held as the Seventh City of Christendom before Napoleonic Paris was built.'

Oliver St John Gogarty, *As I Was Going Down Sackville Street* (1937).

'As long as there is English spoken in the home, whatever is taught in the morning will be undone in the evening by the parents, and the greatest enthusiast has not suggested the shooting of mothers of English-speaking children.'

Oliver St John Gogarty, on the Gaeltacht Commission Report, Seanad Éireann (10 March 1927).

Labour Party

Suprisingly, it was not the ire of the great lockout of 1913 or the fire of the shelling of Liberty Hall in 1916 that gave rise to James Larkin and James Connolly's Labour Party, but a meeting a few years earlier in a shabby hall in that unlikely hotbed of urban class conflict, Clonmel. It was an unconventional start for one of Europe's most un-conventional socialist groupings. Labour has been served by some fiery orators steeped in the tradition of Marx and trade unionism as well as some unlikely champions of the working class, many representing rural areas and holding true to high Church doctrine. Great debates and debaters, splits and make-ups and, almost in equal measure, moments of genius and codology have coloured its history.

'A two-and-a-half-party system.'
Ronan Fanning, UCD professor, on the Labour Party's inability to challenge the two main parties since independence.

'Successful revolutions are not the product of our brains, but of ripe material conditions.'

James Connolly, *Labour in Irish History* (1910).

'The struggle for Irish freedom has two aspects; it is national and it is social. It is social and economic because no matter what the form of the Government may be, as long as one class owns as private property the land and instruments of labour from which mankind derive their substance, that class will always have it in their power to plunder and enslave the remainder of their fellow creatures.'

James Connolly (1910).

'But what is Anarchy? Anarchy means the highest form of love. It means that a man must trust himself and live on himself . . . I am a Socialist. I believe in a co-operative commonwealth, but that is far ahead in Ireland.'

James Larkin, *Larkin's Scathing Indictment of Dublin Sweaters* (1913).

'Independence struggles which are led by the conservative or middle classes, as in Ireland in 1921, tend to compromise with imperialism because their leading sections benefit from such a compromise. That is why those on the left in Ireland who regard themselves as socialists and as representatives of the working class should be the most uncompromising republicans.'

Gerry Adams, *The Politics of Freedom* (1986).

'Governments in a capitalist society are but committees of the rich to manage the affairs of the capitalist class.'

James Connolly, *Irish Worker* (29 August 1914).

'I make no war upon patriotism; never have done. But against the patriotism of capitalism – the patriotism which makes the interest of the capitalist class the supreme test of duty and right – I place the patriotism of the working class, the patriotism which judges every public act by its effect upon the fortunes of those who toil.'

James Connolly, 'A Continental Revolution' (1915).

'There is not a county in the twenty-six counties, there is not a barracks or jail out of which has not come information which is a disgrace to any Irish government.'

Cathal O'Shannon (9 September 1922).

'No country can be strong and healthy on a diet of revolution. A revolution is an emetic, not a food.'

Tom Johnson (3 June 1927).

'Ireland puts the portrait of that great enemy of imperialism, James Connolly, on its postage stamps, but in practice, in the routine conduct of its foreign policy, daily betrays everything that he, Connolly, stood for. This hypocrisy does not make us respected.'

Conor Cruise O'Brien, on joining the Labour Party (19 December 1968).

'Left-wing political queers from Trinity College and Teilifis Éireann.'

Micheál Ó Móráin, Minister for Justice (1969).

'The Labour Party is like the Widow Macree's do, who will go a piece of the road with anyone.'

Gerry Collins, Fianna Fáil frontbencher (5 December 1970).

'Some members of the cabinet would find it difficult ever to agree with me.'
Dick Spring, Labour Party leader, at the annual conference (1984).

'History has dealt a mortal blow to those who gave blind, uncritical support to the Eastern bloc. It is a valid criticism of my party that we did not more publicly criticise the defects we saw. But socialism is not dead. Stalinism is dead.'
Proinsias De Rossa, President of the Workers Party, at the party's Ard Fheis (28 April 1990).

'They told us back in 1917 that Labour must wait. We are not waiting any longer.'
Dick Spring, during the 1992 general election campaign.

'Spring tide.'
Description of Labour's 1992 general election success under party leader Dick Spring when the party won thirty-three Dáil seats.

'Labour will strike a hard bargain.'
Albert Reynolds in mid-campaign (19 November 1992).

'I am against coalition ... this is a matter of conscience and ... in such an eventuality, my continued support for socialism will be from the backbenches.'
Brendan Corish (24 January 1969).

'Now he wants to use this mandate to put back in office the same Taoiseach, the same ministers and the same party against whom he has campaigned with such self-conscious rhetoric for five years. Such a somersault diminishes not only his credibility but the credibility of all politicians.'

John Bruton, eader of Fine Gael, on the Labour Party leader Dick Spring joining a partnership government with Fianna Fáil (5 January 1993).

'It will not be easy for Labour Party members to subscribe to it, for those who support us to accept it. Nor indeed was it easy for us in government to agree to it.'

Dick Spring, speaking before the 1993 budget.

'I kind of like Dick but he's touchy and when he is not being touchy, Fergus is touchy for him.'

Seán Duignan, *One Spin on the Merry-Go-Round* (1995).

'A safe pair of hands!'

Subtitle of book by Tim Ryan about Dick Spring (1993).

'It is not the end of the journey. It is the commencement of a wonderful radical voyage.'

Ruairi Quinn (12 December 1998).

'I didn't get the votes.'

Dick Spring, on why he lost in 2002. In his farewell speech, he quoted Lord Birkenhead, turning to Martin Ferris and saying, 'Am I allowed to quote lords, Martin?'

'Democratic Left has absolutely no principles. They went from Sinn Féin to Official Sinn Féin/IRA to Sinn Féin the Workers Party, the Workers Party, New Agenda and Democratic Left, leaving a trail of destruction in every party they have been a part of. They have no home now so they are prepared to crawl to us.'

Brian Fitzgerald (12 December 1998).

'Jaze, lads, ye're giving us an awful bad name.'

Brian Cowen, on the appointment of Labour supporters to state boards which followed the formation of the coalition government with Fianna Fáil in 1992.

Land:

The Eternal Question

When the entire parliamentary debates archive went online (www.irlgov.ie/oireachtas), one of the big surprises for political anoraks was how much valuable parliamentary time was spend discussing land and the carving up of estates in the early decades of the Dáil. It was one of the most important government ministries, and our elected representatives spent endless hours of fun discussing the townlands of every nook and cranny in the country. Put any townland in the search and it will turn up in a tedious debate about land, who owned it, and who would get it now the tenants were in charge. No wonder the land-commission staff took to writing plays.

'Trí féich nach dlegar faill: féich thíre, duilgine achaid, argius aiste.' ('Three debts which must not be neglected: debts of land, payment of a field, instruction of poetry.')

Kuno Meyer, *The Triads of Ireland* (14th century).

'The principle I state, and mean to stand upon, is this, that the entire ownership of Ireland, moral and material, up to the sun, and down to the centre, is vested of right in the people of Ireland.'

James Fintan Lalor, *Irish Felon* (24 June 1848).

'I think the only true solution of the land question is the abolition of landlordism. The land of Ireland belongs to the people of Ireland.'

John Devoy (October 1878).

'The Free State Government are bound by the most formal and explicit undertaking to continue to pay the land annuities to the National Debt Commissioners, and the failure to do so would be a manifest violation of an engagement which is binding in law and honour on the Irish Free State.'

J.H. Thomas, Dominions Secretary, to Eamon de Valera (23 March 1932).

'Your cousin Dan is fixed up nicely. I saw to that. Fifteen acres of the best of it and bordering his own. I also got ten acres for myself. I have as much right to it as anybody. 'Twas us broke the English yoke.'

John B. Keane, *Letters of a Successful TD* (1967).

'Many of the aliens who come here to purchase land do not know our land history, do not know of the Land Wars, of Parnell, Davitt and Dillon, of the congestion problem which exists to this very day. These people come here not knowing how sacred the land is to the people of Ireland and how treasured it is. That is why I would ask the Minister for Lands to consult with the Minister for External Affairs and with all embassies in this city and ask them to appeal to their countrymen and tell them that the purchase of such land by aliens is strongly resented.'

Oliver J. Flanagan (18 November 1969).

'Who is to be the judge of whether lands are or are not properly utilised? Is it the State? Is it the persons who live in the vicinity? Is it the corner-boy in the local village? Who is to be the judge?'

Connor Hogan, Dáil Éireann (18 June 1925).

Law and Lawyers

The early political leaders used to make the laws as well. The lawyers soon put a stop to that. We haven't found a way of putting a stop to the lawyers ever since. Rows over legal cases have caused most of the political crises of the past decade and a half.

'Trí ata ferr do fhlaith: fír, síth, slóg.' ('Three things that are best for a chief: justice, peace, an army.')

Kuno Meyer, *The Triads of Ireland* (14th century).

'Trí all frisa timargar béscna: mainister, flaith, fine.' ('Three rocks to which lawful behaviour is tied: a monastery, a chieftain, the family.')

Kuno Meyer, *The Triads of Ireland* (14th century).

'Born to little or no fortune of his own, he [Sir Condy Rackrent] was bred to the bar, at which having many friends to push him, and no mean abilities of his own, he doubtless would in process of time, if he could have

borne the drudgery of that study, have been rapidly made king's counsel at the least.'
Maria Edgeworth, *Castle Rackrent* (1800).

'I am not a lawyer, and the ways of lawyers are like the ways of the Heathen Chinese, peculiar and dark.'
Thomas Johnson, Labour Party Leader, Dáil Éireann (13 September 1922).

'People, after all, must live, must order their lives either by law or by the strong hand; by the quick draw on the gun, the light finger and the sure eye; or by rules made by their own representatives in their parliament.'
Kevin O'Higgins, speaking on the Enforcement of Law (Occasional Powers) Bill, Seanad Éireann (8 February 1923).

'The RIC was formerly an army of occupation. Now, owing to the all but complete disappearance of crime, it is an army of no occupation.'
Thomas Kettle.

'This wretched commission, this incompetent, futile, hopeless, obscurantist body wrote the most idiotic report that ever disgraced a body of people that sat round a table to inquire into a grave social problem.'
James Dillon, on the Children's Bill (5 February 1941).

'The courts are open to anyone, like the Ritz.'
Noel Browne (17 July 1971).

'Judge John O'Connor seemed to fall asleep on the Wednesday last: the courtroom is high ceilinged but the well of the court is packed and very stuffy by mid afternoon. At 2.42 p.m. his head was only inches above the bench but three minutes later he sat up and began to write; at 3.10 p.m. his head seems to be actually resting on the bench but two minutes later he again sits up.'

Niall Kelly, report of the Sallins train robbery trial in *Hibernia* (February 1978). Appeals to have the court discharged on the basis that Judge O'Connor was falling asleep were dismissed. After sixty-five days of the trial, Judge O'Connor dropped dead.

'You can't toss a hat into the Dáil without hitting a lawyer, yet we seem to have set up a committee without a single member who has the faintest idea of the rules of evidence or procedure.'

Jack Lynch, conversation with John Peck, British Ambassador (16 February 1971).

'If all this fails: take a deep breath, look the fat barrister straight in the eye and lie.'

Gene Kerrigan, advice on how to succeed in a tribunal, in *Never Make a Promise You Can't Break: How to Succeed in Irish Politics* (2002).

'Certain solicitors in Northern Ireland are unduly sympathetic to one or another terrorist organisation in Northern Ireland.'

Douglas Hogg, British Conservative MP (17 January 1989). Three weeks later, Pat Finucane, a prominent Nationalist lawyer, was assassinated.

'I wish to condemn a statement made by Douglas Hogg recently and we firmly believe that it was instrumental in

Pat's death. I totally refute claims made by the UFF that Pat was a member of the IRA. Patrick was a solicitor who worked for human rights and civil liberties. He defended both Catholic and Protestant alike.'

Geraldine Finucane (13 February 1989).

'Had my colleagues and I been aware of these facts last week, we would not have proposed or supported the nomination of Harry Whelehan as President of the High Court. I now accept that the reservations voiced by the Tánaiste were well founded and I regret the appointment.'

Albert Reynolds, commenting on the extradition request for paedophile priest, Brendan Smyth (17 November 1994).

'The worst threat is that I am going to be killed. Interrogators told one guy, "You're going to die when you get out. And tell Rosemary she's going to die too."'

Rosemary Nelson, a lawyer who represented the Nationalist residents of Garvaghy Road, Portadown, speaking eighteen months before she was killed in a car bomb (1 October 1997).

'Of all the cubs being suckled by the Celtic Tiger, by far the fattest, sleekest and best nurtured are the lawyers.'

Pat Rabbitte (18 December 1997).

'I'm faced with the kind of bill for soldiers in terms of compensation for deafness, that hasn't happened in any other country in the world, even those that were at war. The claims are wrong and immoral, the result of a cancer that is eating away at the heart of our society, fuelled by a greedy minority of solicitors.'

Michael Smith, Minister for Defence, as members of the

army brought 3,000 cases of compensation for alleged hearing loss against the state. Over £65 million was paid out (23 January 1998).

'I did not think I was going to be dealing with half the legal profession of Ireland. I actually thought what I was doing was trying to deal with people who were hard done by.'

Bertie Ahern, on compensation for abuse victims (2002).

'From the dock? Put me in the dock, that's where they want me, in the dock. Oh Jesus, oh Mother of God!'

James Gogarty, at the Flood Tribunal, after Garrett Cooney, Counsel for JMSE, complained about Gogarty's habit of making 'long rambling speeches from the dock' (17 February 1999).

'An increasing number of lawyers are seeing their cases as money-making exercises and running them on the basis of fees.'

Edmund Honohan, Master of the High Court (2005).

'I think that all County Courts in Ireland were built from a single plan in the Office of the Board of Works. Some were smaller and some larger than others; but they reproduced the same discomfort in every country town.'

Maurice Healy, *The Old Munster Circuit: A Book of Memories and Traditions* (1939).

'What has been noticed, and not only by begrudgers, but by every justice and judge sufficiently sober to be aware of what is going on in his court, is that there seems to be no respect at all for the oath in Ireland, and that this has been the case for years.

They are swallowed daily, and not just by plaintiffs, defendants and witnesses but by members of the Garda Síochána as well, as if they were raw eggs and sherry.'

Breandán Ó hEithir, *The Begrudger's Guide to Irish Politics* (1986).

'I sometimes feel that the criminal law in Ireland can be like a game of football with very peculiar rules. The prosecution can score as many goals as they like but the game goes on. As soon as the defence score a goal the game is over and the defence are declared the winner.'

James Hamilton, Director of Public Prosecutions (2006).

'I know what I know.'

Michael McDowell (2004).

'We left the jury to drink itself stupid. But they could never do that if they were drinking to this day, for they were stupid before they started.'

Eric Cross, *The Tailor and Ansty* (1942).

' "Tell me, in your country what happens to a witness who does not tell the truth?" Replies the Irishman, with a candour that disarmed all criticism: I think his side usually wins!"'

Maurice Healy, *The Old Munster Circuit: A Book of Memories and Traditions* (1939).

'Have you ever committed perjury before?'

Kevin O'Higgins, to policeman at his trial for breach of the peace in 1918. When the sergeant admitted that he had not taken down O'Higgins' speech but had made 'mental notes'.

O'Higgins replied, 'I suggest that you had a good deal of blank space for that purpose.' Quoted in Terence de Vere White, *Kevin O'Higgins* (1948).

'I did not give it special priority because I did not identify it as a case which required that priority over other priority work.'

Matt Russell, on why he had the extradition warrants for the paedophile Fr Brendan Smyth on his desk for seven months, hastening the collapse of the Labour–Fianna Fáil Government and leading to the resignation of Albert Reynolds as Taoiseach and leader of Fianna Fáil (1994).

'17th February 1992. The introduction of internment in Ireland for 14-year-old girls.'

Martyn Turner cartoon in *The Irish Times* during the X case.

Seán Lemass

Had de Valera retired in 1948 rather than 1958, it would likely have been Seán MacEntee who succeeded him. Instead it was Seán Lemass who came to the job and transformed the role completely, which suggests Dev knew something the rest of his party didn't. Lemass was master of the sound bite before sound bites were invented, unparalleled spin-doctor before spin-doctors came to weave, and such a champion of his own reputation that he has been treated kindly by supporters, opponents, historians and commentators ever since. Pity the son-in-law didn't pick up a few tips.

'We ask Deputies in this House to co-operate with us in abolishing the memory of past dissensions, in wiping out the recollection of the hatred, the bitterness and the jealousies that were created in this country after the Civil War.'

Seán Lemass, in his maiden speech to Dáil Éireann (11 October 1927).

'Personally I believe that national progress of any kind depends largely on an upsurge of patriotism. Patriotism as

I understand it is a love of country, pride in its history, traditions and culture, and a determination to add to its prestige and achievements.'

Seán Lemass (23 June 1959).

'The historic task of this generation is to secure the economic foundation of independence.'

Seán Lemass, Dáil Éireann (3 June 1959).

'We now see our task as reuniting the Irish people as well as reuniting the Irish territory.'

Seán Lemass (20 October 1963).

'There is among the [people in Northern Ireland] a growing desire to change the present image of that area from a place where time never seemed to move, where old animosities are carefully fostered, and where bigotry and intolerance seem to be preserved as a way of life, to one in closer conformity to the spirit of the age.'

Seán Lemass (12 April 1964).

'I think I can say a roadblock has been removed. How far the road may go is not yet known [but] it is better to travel hopefully than to arrive.'

Seán Lemass, after meeting Terence O'Neill at Stormont (14 January 1965).

'It is time I passed on. I don't want to become a national monument about the place.'

Seán Lemass, announcing his resignation (10 November 1966).

'The devious course which he has pursued, not only in relation to his leadership and on the succession, but to other questions as well, have confounded the members of our organisation so that none of them knows where we stand on any issue.'

Seán MacEntee (9 November 1966).

'Unity has got to be thought of as a spiritual development which will be brought about by peaceful, persuasive means.'

'Seán Lemass Looks Back', *Irish Press* (28 January 1969).

'It was neither his manner of gaining power, nor his manner of holding it, that distinguished him uniquely among Irish prime ministers. It was his manner of using it.'

J.J. Lee, *Ireland 1912–85: Politics and Society* (1989).

'Well, the main difference is that we're in and they're out.'

Seán Lemass (attrib.), when asked what the principal difference between Fianna Fáil and Fine Gael, quoted in Laurence Flanagan, *Irish Humorous Quotations* (1994).

Jack Lynch

The camán-wielding compromise Taoiseach became a near-mystical figure within his own lifetime, probably within his own term of office. In years to come, they will wonder was he real at all, or invented like one of those mythical high kings designed to make everyone feel better about themselves long after they themselves have passed on.

'It is often said he is too straight and honest for his calling.'
Business and Finance magazine, on Jack Lynch (August 1965).

'Honest Jack.'
John Healy, nickname for Lynch, first used by in his column, 'Backbencher' in *The Irish Times*.

'There is not an hour or a day of the week until they break his heart, that the clash of knives will not be heard in the corridors of Fianna Fáil. He is as expendable as an old shoe; and he is too decent a man to be treated in that way. I do not despair that our people will recoil with loathing from the prospect of replacing a man of integrity, as I believe Deputy Jack Lynch to be, with one of the Camorra who are now sharpening their knives and whirling their tomahawks, not only for their enemies but for one another.'

James Dillon, speaking in Dáil Éireann, before the election of Lynch as Taoiseach (11 November 1966).

'Let me make it clear too that in seeking reunification, our aim is not to extend the domination of Dublin. We have many times down the years expressed our willingness to seek a solution on federal lines.'

Jack Lynch (20 September 1969).

'We do not want to seek to impose our will on anyone by force.'

Jack Lynch (22 October 1969).

'The events since the introduction of internment without trial on Monday, 9th of August, clearly indicate the failure of internment and of current military operations as a solution to the problems of Northern Ireland. I intend to support the policy of passive resistance now being pursued by the non-Unionist population.'

Jack Lynch, in a telegram to Edward Heath, British Prime Minister (19 August 1971).

'Urban guerrilla warfare can only work if there is co-operation from the people. This co-operation certainly exists because the minority are looking to the Provisionals for protection.'

Jack Lynch, to Edward Heath, British Prime Minister (September 1971).

'A dialogue of the deaf.'

John Peck, British ambassador in Dublin, speaking on the Lynch/Heath summit (September 1971).

'The time could come when Mr Faulkner and the British Government may have to talk to the IRA instead of the Irish Government.'

Jack Lynch, to Edward Heath and Brian Faulkner at a tripartite summit (27–8 September 1971).

'Mr Heath's assertion that what is happening in Northern Ireland is no concern of mine is not acceptable. The division of Ireland has never been, and is not now, acceptable to the great majority of the Irish people who were not consulted in the matter when that division was made fifty years ago.'

Jack Lynch (20 August 1971).

'Dev ran the cabinet more the way I do. I like to engage everybody around the table like Dev did. I don't count heads. Nowadays we argue it out and eventually I interpret a decision if it has not already become clear-cut. I usually have an idea myself in advance what decision I think is the right one, and this is usually the one that we make, but not always.'

Jack Lynch, on his cabinet style, quoted in Stephen Collins, *The Power Game: Fianna Fáil since Lemass* (2000).

'When the House rises at the conclusion of this debate, it will do so at the end of one of the most successful periods on record for the Irish economy.'

Jack Lynch, Dáil Éireann (14 December 1978).

'The most popular Irish politician since Daniel O'Connell.'

Liam Cosgrave, tribute when Jack Lynch retired as Taoiseach and party leader (5 December 1979).

'There are things he should have known, and he should have exercised more authority over individual members of the government, but he exercised a hands-off approach to his ministers in the knowledge that many of them had more experience than himself and he believed that they would act at all times in the interests of the state.'

Michael Mills, *The Irish Times.*

'When a great statesman passes away it is traditional to ask what political legacy he has left behind him. The Lynch legacy is manifold but, if you want to know his most important legacy, look around you. For the safe existence of this democratic state in which we live today is very much Jack Lynch's legacy. Thirty years ago as a nation we were confronted with a stark choice. We could have caved in to sinister elements and put our country at mortal risk. Jack Lynch chose not to. Confronted with some of the most difficult decisions to face any Taoiseach of the modern era, he took determined and resolute action to defend democracy and to uphold the rule of law. When he came to the crossroads of history thirty years ago, he knew which turn to take. Upon such foundations are freedom and democracy built.'

Desmond O'Malley, oration at Jack Lynch's graveside (1999)

Newspapers and
the Media

One of the earliest Dáil debates was about excluding a newspaper journalist from the chamber for not treating politicians with enough deference. The healthy disregard they hold for each other has continued ever since.

'Newspapers are unable, seemingly, to discriminate between a bicycle accident and the collapse of civilisation.'
George Bernard Shaw.

'But who are the Irish? Not the rack-renting, slum-owning landlord; not the sweating, profit-grinding capitalist; not the sleek and oily lawyer; not the prostitute pressman – the hired liars of the enemy. Not these are the Irish upon whom the future depends.'
James Connolly, *The Irish Flag*.

'That the *Freeman's Journal's* representative be turned out

from this assembly and not re-admitted until the proprietors
and editors of the journal give an undertaking that they will
report what happens here.'

Margaret McSwiney, after *Freeman's Journal* reported that
Dáil speeches were too long-winded to report (5 January
1922).

'Free speech was governed by certain conditions, one of
which was that no party advocating foreign domination was
entitled in any country to misguide the people.'

Irish Press, editorial in the first issue (5 September 1931).

'Be on your guard against the habits of British and foreign
news agencies who look at the world mainly through
imperialist eyes. Tammany is an American institution disliked
by British agencies. Be careful of one-sided accounts of its
activities. Propagandist attacks on Russia and other countries
should not be served up as news. Do not make the *Irish Press*
a Dublin newspaper. There are O'Connell streets in other
cities as well.'

Irish Press, instructions to sub editors on the first issue
(September 1931).

'The *Irish Press,* known as the Fianna Fáil *Pravda.*'

James Dillon speaking in Dáil Éireann (15 November 1951).
He repeatedly described the *Irish Press* as *Pravda* over the
next twenty years.

'We are not the organ of an individual, or a group, or a party.
We are a national organ, in all that term conveys. We have
given ourselves the motto: truth in the news. We shall be
faithful to it. Even the news exposes a weakness of our own,

or a shortcoming in the policies we approve, or a criticism of individuals with whom we are associated, we shall publish it, if its inherent news value so demands.'

Irish Press, editorial, first issue, (5 September 1931).

'We all know that *The Irish Times* is the mistress of the Fine Gael party, and mistresses can be both vicious and demanding.'

Micheál Ó Móráin, Minister for Lands (May 1966).

'Tony O'Reilly had instructed his editors at lunch that no support whatsoever was to be given to Haughey's efforts to return to 'respectability' and [to] the Fianna Fáil front bench.'

Michael Daly, official at British Embassy in Dublin after meeting with Tony O'Reilly (8 January 1975).

'The Government here has freedom from the Press. This is compensated for by the fact that it owns a Press which has no freedom from the Government . . .'

Oliver St John Gogarty, *As I was going down Sackville Street*

'Payback time'

Irish Independent headline on election day (1997).

'A very fine journalist, an excellent man, but on Northern questions a renegade or white nigger.'

Andrew Gilchrist, British ambassador in a letter to Kelvin White of the UK Foreign and Commonwealth Office's Western European Department, commenting on *The Irish Times* editor Douglas Gageby (2 October 1969). He attributed the remarks to Major Tom McDowell, but McDowell denied making them.

'Journalism is the modern equivalent of the priesthood. Just as the child and adolescent was cared for in the education system, the adult is delivered by the newspapers.'

Noel Browne, interview in *Magill* magazine (1987).

'I'll give you a copy of the medical report on Brian Lenihan if you give me a copy of a medical report on Vincent Browne.'

P.J. Mara speaking to a *Sunday Tribune* reporter querying the physical health of Brian Lenihan (14 November 1989).

'Well you got it wrong didn't you.'

Charles Haughey, to reporters covering coup attempt against him (10 November 1990).

'Dick Spring has the media wind at his back. I used to call *Morning Ireland* 'Good Morning, Dick'. If there was a change in the weather, they rang him.'

Eamon Gilmore Democratic Left TD, on the Labour Party leader's exposure on RTÉ (4 December 1992).

'It has been said of Goldhawk that, apart form the DPP, he has been the cause of the employment of more lawyers than any other person in Ireland.'

Paddy Prendiville writing in the tenth anniversary edition of *Phoenix* magazine (April 1993).

'The fabric of Irish society has been badly damaged. The death of *Irish Press* newspapers is not just the end of an era in Irish journalism, it is a tragedy for those who sought an alternative voice and those who provided it.'

Michael Keane, editor of *Irish Press* (24 May 1995).

Progressive Democrats

The mantle of the fourth-largest political party has been passed around rather merrily over the decades. The Farmer's Party, which supported the government in the 1920s was, at one stage, bigger than Labour. The Centre Party of 1933 merged into Fine Gael. Michael Donnellan and Joe Blowick's Clann na Talmhan of the 1940s also passed Labour before disappearing. Seán MacBride's Clann na Poblachta had fewer TDs but made more impact that Clann na Talmhan thanks to its succession of by-election victories and the strength of the personalities MacBride brought to the cabinet table. The Workers' Party emerged to become Democratic Left and join Labour, and the Greens captured the environmental concerns of a new generation. But one party has had an impact far beyond its numbers. It all started in 1986, when they threw Desmond O'Malley out of Fianna Fáil.

'There is no one available to answer your call but please leave a message after the high moral tone.'

Telephone-answering-machine joke of 1987, after the Progressive Democrats came into being.

'Progressive Desocrats.'

Nickname for Progressive Democrats, punning on party leader and founder Desmond O'Malley, *Phoenix* magazine (1986).

'We are no good making tea.'

Mary Harney commentating on proposals that the Progressive Democrats and Fianna Fáil form a coalition (2002).

'Progressive Democrats – these are very principled people, except when their political or personal interests are at stake.'

Gene Kerrigan, *Never Make a Promise You Can't Break: How to Succeed in Irish Politics* (2002).

'Des O'Malley was reduced to sleeping under political bridges.'

John Kelly TD, commenting on O'Malley after his expulsion from Fianna Fáil, quoted in Dick Walsh, *Des O'Malley* (1986).

'A crowd of cut calves.'

Frank McLoughlin TD, remarking about the foundation of the Progressive Democrats (January 1987).

'The politics would be, to be one of the lads, the safest way in Ireland. But I do not believe that the interests of this state, or our constitution and of this republic would be served by putting politics before conscience in regard to this. There is a choice of a kind that can only be answered by saying that I stand by the republic and accordingly I will not oppose this Bill.'

Desmond O'Malley (20 February 1985). He voted against the Fianna Fáil party line on family planning and was expelled from the party by seventy-three votes to nine on 26 February 1985.

'Smog and Smug.'

Nicknames for Mary Harney and Padraig Flynn during Harney's campaign to rid Dublin city of smog and the testy relationship with Flynn, who was senior minister in the same department.

'The PDs are like Mao Zedong. He believed in perpetual revolution. They believe in perpetual negotiation.'

John Bruton (16 October 1991).

'A temporary little arrangement.'

Albert Reynolds (1991).

'What about the PDs? When in doubt, leave out.'

Brian Cowen speaking to the Fianna Fáil Ard Fheis (1992).

'The Progressive Democrats should be called The Old Man River Party. They're afraid of living and scared of dying.'

Pat Rabbitte (May 1998).

'The prospect of Fianna Fáil examining the impact of the Maastricht Protocol on the Irish Constitution is like a chimpanzee with a screwdriver at the back of a television set.'

Michael McDowell (1994).

'It is very difficult to remain in government if the leader of one party in effect charges the leader of the other party in the same Government with perjury. We don't want to be in government for the sake of sitting at a desk.'

Desmond O'Malley (3 November 1992).

'Fianna Fáil itself is a bit of a rainbow.'

Mary Harney speaking during the 1992 general election campaign.

'The amendment was the predictable consequence of running the country out of the hip pocket and handbag of coalition leaders without consultation or reflection.'

Michael McDowell (18 October 1997).

'An enterprise economy is what creates an inclusive society.'

Mary Harney (27 July 1999).

'The Progressive Democrats are still the only party that preaches a liberal philosophy on economic issues. And we are still the only party that promotes competition right across all sectors of the economy as a matter of political principle.'

Mary Harney (23 October 2003).

'I want to apologise to the pony.'

Mary Harney, after hitching a ride on a pony and trap on a visit to Laois-Offaly during the general election campaign (28 April 2002).

'I have grown increasingly uneasy in recent times at the way in which the Progressive Democrats are melting back into Fianna Fáil. The party now lacks the hunger and energy to fight for its relevance in this very unbalanced government, where the domineering Fianna Fáil party has killed off any chance that the Progressive Democrats had to make an impact.

Helen Keogh, in her resignation statement (13 June 2000).

'Stop single-party government.'
Mary Harney, during 2002 election campaign.

'Well it depends on what kind of loaf of bread you buy. I don't
particularly buy loaves of bread, I buy little brown cakes. But
you can pay anything from 30p up. I suppose one of the
concerns I have for milk is that farmers get so little for milk
and we pay so much for it in the retail sector.'
Mary Harney, responding to a question on the price of a loaf
of bread during the 2002 gneral election campaign.

There were opened toed sandals on the pavement, there was
museli in the air'
Michael McDowell accuses Green Party supporters of riotous
behaviour

'Goebbels.'
Michael McDowell, talking about Fine Gael's Richard Bruton (2006).

'Was it for this that the Tánaiste flew to the tops of the
lamp-posts all over Dublin to tell us we needed him in
government to straighten out the Fianna Fáil chancers? The
lamp-posts will be left to the poodles of Ranelagh to do at
the base what the Tánaiste is doing today to the alleged
standards he defended when he climbed up on his ladders.'
Joe Higgins, Dáil Éireann (3 October 2006).

'Deputy McDowell is trying to work hard to have us believe
he has no previous history in government, that he has not been
in government for ten years, and that he has no responsibility for the billions of euro in stamp duty and the rest.

He wants us to believe he is a political newborn, dropped by a stork, perhaps, into a basket outside Government Buildings two weeks ago, with Deputy O'Donnell playing along as the besotted nurse fetchingly referring to him as Michael, if one does not mind. That is somewhat different from the name she was spitting out two months ago from behind clenched teeth, when Michael was trying to take the PD rattler from Mary.'

Joe Higgins, Dáil Éireann (27 September 2006).

Peace and
the Peace Process

The winning of peace in 1994 was one of the great turning points of Irish history. It makes one wonder how many lives could have been saved if the politicians had not meddled in all the previous peace initiatives.

'There is a parable about the fox and the hedgehog . . . The hedgehog, according to the story, knows one big thing; the fox knows many things. In terms of this story, John Hume is the hedgehog, who knew the big truth that justice had to prevail. David Trimble is the fox, who has known many things but who had the intellectual clarity and political courage to know that 1998 was the time to move Unionism forward.'

Seamus Heaney (17 October 1998).

'When this euphoria of the Nationalist community wore off, as it inevitably did, the minority were left with no clear sense of the remarkable number of changes effected through its mechanisms, and as a result the longer run impact of the agreement among Nationalists was much less than we intended, although it was clearly sufficient to consolidate the drop in IRA support that had begun while it was under negotiation.'

Garret FitzGerald, on the Anglo-Irish Agreement, *All in a Life: An Autobiography* (1991).

'I always thought that the people of the Falls and the people of the Shankill were just the same. Now I know.'

Mairead Corrigan (29 August 1976).

'Our purpose is to secure equal recognition and respect for the two identities in Northern Ireland. Nationalists can now raise their heads knowing their position is and is seen to be on an equal footing with that of members of the Unionist community.'

Garret FitzGerald, speaking at signing of Anglo-Irish Agreement (15 November 1985).

'I went into this agreement because I was not prepared to tolerate a situation of continuing violence. I believe in the Union and that it will last as long as the majority so wish.'

Margaret Thatcher (15 November 1985).

'If in fact the terrorists were to decide that the moment had come when they wished to withdraw from their activities, then I think that Government would need to be imaginative . . . in how it responded. Let me remind you of the move towards independence in Cyprus and a British minister stood up and used the word "never" ... in two years there had been a retreat from that word.'

Peter Brooke, Northern Ireland Secretary of State (November 1989).

'Mr Brooke's refusal to rule out future talks with Sinn Féin is a public admission of the inevitability of such talks. Sinn Féin is ready at any time to discuss the conditions in which justice and peace can be established.'

Gerry Adams (6 November 1989).

'Britain will not leave Northern Ireland until after a sustained period of peace. Sinn Féin is not standing in the airport lounge waiting to be flown to Chequers or Lancaster House. Idealists we are, fools we are not.'

Jim Gibney, speaking at the Bodenstown commemoration (June 1992), This speech was regarded as a significant move towards the peace process.

'Demography is all, uncertainty breeds insecurity, insecurity breeds violence.'

Opsahl Report (1993).

'The process called for a risk-taker and Albert Reynolds was certainly that.'

Martin Mansergh, quoted in Seán Duignan, *One Spin on the Merry-Go-Round* (1995).

'My attendance at the funeral of Mr Begley has been a matter of some controversy. My absence would have had the same effect.'

Gerry Adams (27 October 1993).

'I think sometimes we are too reluctant to engage ourselves in a positive way [in Northern Ireland] because of our long-standing special relationship with Great Britain and also because it seemed such a thorny problem. But in the aftermath of the Cold War we need a governing rationale for our engagement in the world, not just in Northern Ireland.'
Bill Clinton (5 April 1992).

'The most significant thing I should be doing now is encouraging the resumption of dialogue between the Irish and British governments.'
Bill Clinton (17 March 1993).

'You're on your own, Albert.'
Dick Spring's reaction to Reynolds's attempt to bring the IRA into dialogue, quoted in Seán Duignan, *One Spin on the Merry-Go-Round* (1995).

'The Hume-Adams report does not exist.'
Albert Reynolds to Seán Duignan (7 October 1993). Quoted in Seán Duignan, *One Spin on the Merry-Go-Round* (1995).

'Go the extra mile.'
Bill Clinton, US President, in conversation with John Major (30 November 1993).

'In my view Gerry Adams was a brave man and I hope he will be justified. He led them across the Rubicon. In my view that was a courageous step. The whole world is grateful to him for having done it.'
Peter Brooke (30 January 1995).

'The peace process is like a bicycle. It topples over if it goes too slowly.'

Anthony Lake, US National Security Adviser, to President Clinton (19 May 1995).

'When you strip away the verbiage from the Sinn Féin position, all we are talking about is Sunningdale for slow learners.'

Seamus Mallon (1 April 1997).

'She touched up ultra-Unionists in a way that their wives never did.'

Julia Langdon, Mo Mowlam's biographer, on *Morning Ireland* (11 September 2000).

Politician's Primer

There is no shortage of advice to aspiring politicians from those who have spent a little longer trudging the corridors of power than is altogether healthy.

'Politics is rough, tough, hard. And it will never be any other way. You will never get the views and policies you would like to see done. There is far too much compromise and games to be played. You have to carry too many things with you. There are too many knockers, too many people who are looking for holes in what you do.'

Bertie Ahern (1986).

'Whenever a camera points at you, think hard about a real problem. Focus on it. Nod imperceptibly as you solve it. Let them see you do it.'

Eoghan Harris, campaign advice document to Mary Robinson (6 April 1990). Quoted in Emily O'Reilly, *Candidate: The Truth Behind the Presidential Campaign* (1991).

'Once upon a time it was easy being an Irish politician. All you had to do was let an occasional howl out of you. Something to do with getting the Brits out of the fourth green field would do. Or how the young people were letting us all down by not speaking the first official language or how television would land us all in hell, so it would. Or how the communists would turn us all into Russians if we didn't drive them out of the trade unions.'

Gene Kerrigan, *Never Make a Promise You Can't Break: How to Succeed in Irish Politics* (2002).

'Nobody ever won an election on pity. Only by promising an end to the need for it.'

Eoghan Harris, quoted in Emily O'Reilly, *Candidate: The Truth Behind the Presidential Campaign* (1991).

'If the other side don't ask the right questions, they don't get the right answers. It is not for me to lead them as to where they figure they want to go.'

Ray Burke, explaining the secrets of ministerial office to the Beef Tribunal.

'The force that drives politicians is more primal than principled. It is about getting into office, staying in office and hanging on to power, or what the political world regards as power. The curious thing is that even though the electorate understands this, although that doesn't stop it getting its hopes up and letting past disappointments fade in the collective memory.'

Frank Dunlop, *Yes Taoiseach: Irish Politics from Behind Closed Doors* (2004).

'For most people in rural Ireland, political allegiance is a matter of faith, not of belief. It is the allegiance itself, rather than the cause, that is important. The divide of Irish politics, Fine Gael versus Fianna Fáil, has its roots in the Civil War, but it is the divide itself, rather than the war, that is the significant element.'

John Waters, *Jiving at the Crossroads* (1991).

'Politics is about winning votes, it's not how you perform in Dáil Éireann.'

Fine Gael candidate, quoted in *The Irish Times* during the 2002 general election.

'The only thing I've found out is that there is a lot of blackmail in politics, in getting elected. For example, one man phoned me and said, "If you could get me that planning permission, there's ten votes in my family for you."'

Dr Moosajee Bhamjee (14 May 1997).

'You go out to work from Monday to Saturday and achieve a hundred things. And if you make a mistake on the hundredth thing, that's the issue that's always whacked up. And you get it back from your colleagues. You get it back from the organisation. And you get it back from the public. And I think you can take that for a certain length of time. But you cannot do it for a lifetime. I could not anyway.'

Bertie Ahern (1986).

'There's bound to be a wake tonight and I'll have to put in an appearance. 'Twould cost me fifty number ones if I didn't show up but, by God, although I've done a lot of things in my time I've never missed a funeral. Here's a bit of advice for you.

'If you must go to a funeral make sure you are seen at it. Go well up on front of the hearse and look as solemn as if it 'twas your own mother was being put under.'

John B. Keane, *Letters of a Successful TD* (1967).

'Study economics and read *The Prince*.'

Eamon de Valera, giving advice to Richard Mulcahy on pursuing a political career (3 February 1919). Quoted in Tim Pat Coogan, *De Valera* (1993).

'We'll all wind up like that if we hang around long enough. The odds on anyone surviving in this business are less than on McGlinchey surviving in his.'

Albert Reynolds, on the assassination of former INLA chief Dominic McGlinchey (10 February 1994). Quoted in Seán Duignan, *One Spin on the Merry-Go-Round* (1995).

'Don't ever judge a politician outright if he does something which seems underhand. He is only doing his best to survive.'

John B. Keane, *Letters of a Successful TD* (1967).

'When you get to the top in politics you stop plotting and the minute you stop plotting you start going down.

Katie Hannon, *The Naked Politician* (2004).

'The most effective word in your armoury is real. You deal with real people, in a real way and, unlike left-wing pinko critics who live in an airy fairy utopia, you live in the real world.'

Gene Kerrigan, *Never Make a Promise You Can't Break: How to Succeed in Irish Politics* (2002).

'Politicians' real focus is the pursuit of power. Politics is honourable but hypocritical, honest but full of dissemblers, disinterested but riven in self-interest, forward-looking but caught in a time warp.'

Frank Dunlop, *Yes Taoiseach: Irish Politics from Behind Closed Doors* (2004).

'Internal party strife is a given. Party unity is a fiction.'

Katie Hannon, *The Naked Politician* (2004).

'When it comes to governing under democratic conditions you have either to reduce the people to your own level of mediocrity or reduce yourself to theirs. As a rule it is a compromise which brings both to a lower level than either held.'

Oliver St John Gogarty, *As I Was Going Down Sackville Street* (1937).

'The most popular speaker is the one who sits down before he stands up.'

John Pentland Mahaffy, quoted in W.B. Stanford and R.B. McDowell, *Mahaffy: A Biography of an Anglo-Irishman* (1971).

Presidents and the Presidency

The role of the president in the 1937 Constitution was rife for outrageous populism, meaningless rhetoric and unrealistic waffle. It took a while for the politicians to work it out, but, since then, some of the most successful spinning in the history of the state has taken place during the presidential election when, all too rarely, we get a chance to vote..

'I hasten to make my apologies to you, sincerely and humbly, in this letter. I wish to tender to you my very deep regret for my use of the words "thundering disgrace" in relation to you.'
Paddy Donegan (19 October 1976).

'The gravamen of your utterance is, "In my opinion, he is a thundering disgrace." These words, I find, are followed by the sentence, "The fact is that the Army must stand behind the State." Can this sequence be construed by ordinary people otherwise than as an insinuation that the President does not stand behind the State?'

President Cearbhall Ó Dálaigh (19 October 1976).

'It was amazing when the President sent the Emergency Powers Bill to the Supreme Court. In my opinion he is a thundering disgrace. The fact is that the Army must stand behind the State.'

Paddy Donegan, Minister for Defence, to army officers at Columb Barracks, Mullingar (18 October 1976). According to the only journalist present, Don Lavery, 'thundering' was the word used, despite rumours it was another expletive.

'The Minister for Defence did not attack our institutions, he made what he and I regard as a serious comment on what the President did in a disrespectful way. The extent of his apology demonstrates his regret.'

Liam Cosgrave, resisting calls that Donegan be asked to resign (21 October 1976).

'The only way now open to me is to assert publicly my personal integrity and independence as President of Ireland – a matter of much greater importance for every citizen – to endeavour to protect the dignity and independence of the presidency as an institution, is to resign.'

President Cearbhall Ó Dálaigh (22 October 1976).

'Oh yeah, I mean I got through to him. I remember talking to him and he wanted us to lay off. There was no doubt about it in his mind. In fact, looking back on it, it was a mistake on our part because Paddy Hillery would be very, what's the word, strict or conventional in that way. He wouldn't want to start breaking new ground. He's not that sort of man. He's a very cautious man, the sort of fellow who wouldn't. It didn't break new ground. But of course Charlie was gung ho.'

Brian Lenihan, to MA student Jim Duffy, on telephoning President Hillery after the government collapsed on 27 January 1982 (17 May 1990). Lenihan claimed in his book *For the Record* (1991) that he was on heavy medication when he gave the interview.

Garret FitzGerald: 'Why were there phone calls to try and force [the president] to exercise [the option of refusing to dissolve the Dáil]?'

Brian Lenihan: 'That is a fiction of Garret's.'

Garret FitzGerald: 'Excuse me, it is not a fiction, I was in the Áras that evening and I know how many phone calls there were.'

Exchange on *Questions and Answers* television programme (21 October 1990).

'Other people may have rung the President about what was going to happen now, but I had nothing to do with it, good, bad or indifferent.'

Brian Lenihan (23 October 1990).

'I must have been mistaken in what I said to Jim Duffy on that occasion. It was a casual discussion with a research student and I was obviously mistaken in what I said. What I am saying to you now, Seán [Duignan] and I am telling the Irish public now, is that, on mature recollection, and full reflection, I did not ring President Hillery on that night.'

Brian Lenihan (25 October 1990).

'Whoever told me to look straight at the camera when I said that was wrong.'
Brian Lenihan, *For the Record* (1991).

'Is the Left Right for the Park?'
Fianna Fáil slogan, during the 1990 presidential election campaign.

'She was pretty well constructed in this campaign by her handlers, the Labour Party and the Workers' Party. Of course it doesn't always suit if you get labelled a socialist, because that's a very narrow focus in this country – so she has to try and have it both ways. She has to have new clothes and her new look and her new hairdo and she has the new interest in her family, being a mother and all that kind of thing. But none of you know, none of us who knew Mrs Robinson very well in previous incarnations ever heard her claiming to be a great wife and mother.'
Padraig Flynn, on the RTÉ *Saturday View* programme (2 November 1990).

'That's outrageous and desperate.'
Brendan Howlin, reacting to Flynn's comments on the RTÉ *Saturday View* programme (2 November 1990).

'You are a disgrace. It's about time you had manners. It's disgusting.'
Michael McDowell, reacting to Flynn's comments on the RTÉ *Saturday View* programme, regarded by some as being crucial in drawing attention to the enormity of what Flynn had said (2 November 1990).

'Even as I salute my supporters as Mary Robinson, I must also bid them farewell as President Elect. I was elected by men and women of all parties and none. And above all by Mná na hÉireann, who instead of rocking the cradle, rocked the system. I am not just a president of those here today but of those who cannot be here; and there will always be a light on in Áras an Uachtaráin for our exiles and emigrants.'

Mary Robinson (9 November 1990).

'May it be a presidency where I, the President, can sing to you, citizens of Ireland, the joyous refrain of the fourteenth-century Irish poet as recalled by W.B. Yeats: "I am of Ireland, come dance with me in Ireland."'

Mary Robinson (3 December 1990).

'By 1990 in Ireland we'd been adolescents for seventy years / Obsessed with the Virgin, automobiles, alcohol, Playboy, Unity. / The Commander-in-Chief issued her first and only commandment: / First and last you must learn to love your different self.'

Paul Durcan, on Mary Robinson, 'The First and Last Commandment of the Commander-in-Chief' (1999).

'Fianna Fáil still seem to see the office as a preserve . . . redolent of top hats, motorcades, museum openings and the odd distant wave from a passing limousine. Far from shutting our president up, we should be showing her off.'

John Bruton (17 June 1991).

'Every campaign has one or two Beechers Brooks for some reason. The first is always political. The other is always personal. Now you can't mess around with this. Either you deal with it up front or it is no use even starting this campaign. What you have here is a Jack Kennedy problem. And you have a John F. Kennedy solution as well. Your very first press conference must deal with distortion in a frank and firm fashion as follows: "Now I want to make something clear. Everybody knows my position on divorce and abortion. But that was Mary Robinson's position. As President my private view doesn't count. As President I will fully accept the views of the electorate expressed at the referenda. On this I compare my position to John F. Kennedy – as President of Ireland I represent the views of the people of Ireland. On every issue. Including divorce and abortion. As President my private views don't count." You must say that every chance you get for a whole week and you will never have to say it again. If you don't say it first, and without fidgets and without fiddling, you are a non-runner in this race.'

Eoghan Harris, campaign advice document to Mary Robinson (6 April 1990). Quoted in Emily O'Reilly, *Candidate: The Truth Behind the Presidential Campaign* (1991).

'I had in mind all our exiles, all our emigrants – past and present – when I left the light in the window at Áras an Uachtaráin.'

Mary Robinson (8 July 1992).

'I have to shave in the morning.'

Derek Nally, presidential candidate, when asked what single characteristic set him apart from other four candidates for presidency (2 October 1997).

'Our dancers, singers, writers, poets, musicians, sportsmen and women are giants on the world stage. Our technologically skilled young people are in demand everywhere. There are those who absorb the rush of newness with delight.

There are those who are more cautious, even fearful. I want to point the way to a reconciliation of these many tensions.'
President Mary McAleese, inaugural address (11 November 1997).

'I may not be President but I am a precedent.'
Dana Rosemary Scallon, third-placed presidential candidate (11 November 1997).

'Ooh, she's much better looking than ours.'
New Yorker commenting on Mary McAleese (17 March 2002).

Referenda

True or false, some of the angriest electoral contests in Irish history have been referenda on largely meaningless points of principle which affect the real lives of very few people. Vote yes or no according to preference.

'Hello Divorce, Bye-Bye Daddy.'
Anti-divorce slogan devised by former *Evening Press* deputy features editor Paddy Madden (1996).

'The State acknowledges the right to life of the unborn and, with due regard to the equal right to life of the mother, guarantees in its laws to respect, and, as far as practicable, by its law to defend and vindicate that right.'
Article 40.31 of the Constitution of Ireland.

'The vote, I thought, means nothing to women. We should be armed.'
Edna O'Brien, epigraph to Erica Jong, *Fear of Flying* (1974).

'Could it be that the Government have unwittingly created a constitutional Frankenstein which may sleep for a while and then rise and stalk the land?'

Michael Woods, Minister for Health (14 May 1986).

'Where a marriage has failed the court may in accordance with law grant a dissolution of the marriage provided proper provision will be made for any dependent spouse and for any child.'

Proposed constitutional amendment (16 June 1986).

'Just as the 1925 Boundary Commission reinforced the geographical division of Ireland as negotiated in the 1922 Treaty, the result of the divorce referendum has underpinned the whole concept of partition.'

Desmond O'Malley (8 July 1986).

'G'way, ye wife-swapping sodomites.'

Una Bean Ni Mhathuna, anti-divorce campaigner at a counting centre (26 November 1995).

'Keep your rosaries off our ovaries.'

Pro-choice campaigner (7 March 1997).

'It remains the Government's firm position that there is no need for a referendum on the Partnership for Peace. No other country, not even Switzerland, has had a referendum – and they have one most weekends.'

Bertie Ahern (June 1998).

'Too many people remain confused.'

Pat Egan (88), the country's longest-serving presiding officer, ponders the abortion referendum (5 March 2002).

'The present crowd look like they would make a mess out of a referendum on giving away free fivers.'

Breandán Ó hEithir, comment in wake of abortion (1983) and divorce (1986) referenda, in *The Begrudger's Guide to Irish Politics* (1986).

'Ah, Ireland . . . That damnable, delightful country, where everything that is right is the opposite of what it ought to be.'

Benjamin Disraeli.

Albert Reynolds

The legend of Albert Reynolds was already well established soon after his retirement from politics, partly as a result of his achievements with the Northern Ireland peace process and with the pre-Tiger incubation of the economy, but largely because so many of his private moments came into the public domain so quickly through the investigations of parliamentary committee and the memoirs of Government Press Secretary Seán Duignan and his Labour Party counterpart Frank Finlay.

'I operate a department on the basis of no long files, no long reports; put it on a single sheet and, if I need more information, I know where to get it . . . the one-sheet approach has got me through life very successfully in business and in politics.'

Albert Reynolds, giving evidence to the Beef Tribunal (1992).

'I'm a dealer. Not a wheeler dealer or a double dealer. Just a dealer. That's what I do, hard straight dealing. And that's what I think I can pull off on the north, something they'll all accept as an even deal.'

Albert Reynolds, quoted in Seán Duignan, *One Spin on the Merry-Go-Round* (1995).

'Albert never walked past an open microphone in his life.'

John Major, *An Autobiography* (1999).

'If we haven't got the razor-edged salesmen on the coal face, nobody's going to bring home the beef.'

Albert Reynolds (7 July 1987).

'I will work day and night, go anywhere with any of my colleagues, to work out that new path for peace.'

Albert Reynolds (16 February 1992).

'I've a lot of respect for the dogs in the street. They're customers of mine from time to time.'

Albert Reynolds, speaking to the Public Accounts Committee, when it was put to him that even 'the dogs in the street' knew of the existence and extent of bogus non-resident accounts (September 1999).

'The Taoiseach has been totally vindicated and the tribunal repeatedly emphasises that he at all times acted in the national interest.'

Seán Duignan, Government Press Secretary, in a statement referring to then-unpublished report of the Beef Tribunal (29 July 1994).

'You are the bad guys. Bad Europeans. Bad partners. Bad everything. The game here is for the rest of us to gang up on the anti-EC Brits.

But I think you and I are going to do business.'

Albert Reynolds, to the newly appointed Chancellor of the Exchequer John Major, at an Ecofin meeting (1989). Quoted in Seán Duignan, *One Spin on the Merry-Go-Round* (1995).

'For some time now there has been considerable political instability which has led to an erosion of confidence in our democratic institutions. This uncertainty must not be allowed to continue.'

Albert Reynolds (7 November 1991).

'Now you see the difference between me and other politicians. I believe in life after politics.'

Albert Reynolds (29 October 1993).

'We have an opportunity for peace. Let's maximise it. History will never forgive us if we don't.'

Albert Reynolds (7 November 1993).

'If it comes to it I will walk away from John Major. I am not prepared to let this opportunity pass.'

Albert Reynolds (7 November 1993).

'Everyone says the talks must produce a political settlement before we have peace. Well I am going to put the cart before the horse. We could be talking for another twenty-five years, reach no agreement and still be no nearer an end to violence. So my instinct is peace first, then we can all sit around discussing the new Ireland, but with no one being killed while we are at it.'

Albert Reynolds (4 May 1993). Quoted in Seán Duignan, *One Spin on the Merry-Go-Round* (1995).

'It shows a frightful political immaturity . . . to vote Charles Haughey out of office and take it on for himself is going to wreck our party right down the centre. It's going to bust up Government.'

Gerry Collins (7 November 1991).

'When Albert Reynolds talks about political stability, that seems to me very much like a bookie complaining about gambling.'

Charles J. Haughey (9 November 1991).

'He [Desmond O'Malley] puffed up Goodman's claim for what I regard as cheap political gain. He was reckless, irresponsible and dishonest to do that here at the tribunal.'

Albert Reynolds, Beef Tribunal (29 October 1992).

'Charlie McCreevy is looking at the whole system, to dehumanise it.'

Albert Reynolds, speaking on RTÉ radio (15 November 1992).

'In the course of the interview Reynolds called John Bruton John Unionist – he had been describing him as a crypto-unionist – and he described the Belfast newspaper the *Irish News* as the *Belfast News*. Then, unaccountably, speaking of Charlie McCreevy's objectives, he said he was trying to dehumanise the social-welfare system. Joe Little intervened, "To humanise it, surely?" Reynolds seemed not to hear, "To dehumanise it, yes, to take it away from any harshness that's in it." Afterwards, back in his apartment, he was mystified when I brought up the subject – he was not aware that he had made mistakes – and it took me several minutes to convince him that they had occurred.

I never saw him so dispirited. He said to Kathleen, "It's just that I am so tired."'
Seán Duignan (15 November 1992), Ouoted in Seán Duignan, *One Spin on the Merry-Go-Round* (1995).

'I just can't take it . . . I can't recognise the man I married in what's being said about him. In three weeks he's gone from being the best man around to someone none of us recognise.'
Kathleen Reynolds, on the election trail (16 November 1992). Quoted in Seán Duignan, *One Spin on the Merry-Go-Round* (1995).

'If we in this part of the island appear to walk away from constitutional Nationalism, by unilaterally abandoning our long-standing position with regard to Northern Ireland, the only form of Nationalism left in entire possession of the field is a violent form of Nationalism, which we all repudiate.'
Albert Reynolds (April 1993).

'No pussy-footing. I haven't devoted two years of my life to this to be insulted with a temporary ceasefire. And another thing. I want their announcement to be written in language that an eleven-year-old can understand.'
Albert Reynolds (28 August 1994).

'When I became leader of Fianna Fáil and Taoiseach I set myself two political objectives, to achieve peace in Northern Ireland and on the whole island and to turn the economy around. I was fortunate in such a short space of time to achieve those two political objectives.'
Albert Reynolds, resignation speech (17 November 1994).

'The great point about my relationship with Albert Reynolds was that we liked one another and could have a row without giving up on each other.'

John Major, *An Autobiography* (1999).

'God, Dick, we must be mad to be in this job when we have to meet like this in an airport in the middle of the night. It's no way to live.'

Albert Reynolds, meeting with Dick Spring at Baldonnel Aerodrome at 2 a.m. (11 October 1994). Quoted in Seán Duignan, *One Spin on the Merry-Go-Round* (1995).

'It is unjust and immoral to win on the substantial issue of the case and then for somebody to ask you to pay the costs of the person you defeated.'

Albert Reynolds, after his victory in *The Sunday Times* libel case.

'I am what I am. I do not pretend to be something that I am not. We all have human feelings but we have a good sense of values as well. It was those values that I came into political life to develop. I have stood by values of loyalty and honesty throughout my political life. I leave this morning to go to Áras an Uachtaráin safe in the knowledge that I have lived that kind of political life. That is all I want to be remembered for. I was straight up, I have never hidden anything. Give it as it was; tell it as it is, that is me. That is what I have been and what I always will be. That is the only image I want to leave in the House and in politics.'

Albert Reynolds, in his resignation speech in Dáil Éireann (17 November 1994).

'In life, in business and politics, you cannot win them all. You win some, you lose some but throughout my life in politics and business I have been delighted to be a risk taker. If you are not a risk taker you will not achieve anything. The easiest way in life is not to be a risk taker. Yes, I was a risk taker in politics and business but I am quite happy that, having taken the risks, the successes far outweigh the failures.'

Albert Reynolds, giving his resignation speech in Dáil Éireann(17 November 1994).

'Zero costs.'

Foreman of the jury in the Albert Reynolds's libel trial stating the amount of damages that should be awarded to the former Taoiseach.

'I said to John Major: "How can I go to the Republican leadership and ask them to give up their guns, when Fianna Fáil never handed over any guns?"'

Albert Reynolds (11 August 1997).

'They think they're dealing with the King of Lesotho.'

Dermot Nally, Secretary to the government, on John Major's talks with Albert Reynolds during peace negotiations (1993). Quoted in Seán Duignan, *One Spin on the Merry-Go-Round* (1995).

Albert Reynolds: 'Would you deny me my hour in the sun?'

Dick Spring: 'There may be no sun, Albert. This is bad.'

Aftermath of Beef Tribunal Report (30 July 1994). Quoted in Seán Duignan, *One Spin on the Merry-Go-Round* (1995).

'When Dick Spring called at 2.00 a.m. to break it off I was left shaken. For about four minutes I dropped myself back down on the pillow and said hell. Within about five minutes I was down in my office and back on the phone ringing around the ministers'

Albert Reynolds, speaking of events of 18 November 1994

'This is women now! You can't even give way to somebody who wants to give you information.'

Albert Reynolds, in Dáil exchange with Nora Owen TD (often misquoted as 'There's women for you') (9 December 1993).

Satirists

Politicians are not ones to praise the art of political satire. But then, their more outlandish displays outdo anything the real satirists can come up with.

'We're pathetic really, we don't have snakes, we don't have extreme weather, we don't have a foreign policy, how can we have satire?'

Ardal O'Hanlon, comedian and son of politician Rory O'Hanlon, quoted in Stephen Dixon and Deirdre Falvey, *Gift of the Gab: The Explosion in Irish Comedy* (1999).

'We are now approaching Aldergrove Airport, Belfast. Please put your watches back 300 years.'

Jimmy Young, comedian (1970).

'Anyone who thinks that the events in Northern Ireland are a matter of laughter is a hypocrite.'

Eamonn McCann, Dublin's Peacock Theatre, protesting at the portrayal of Northern Ireland in a satirical revue, *A State of Chassis* (16 September 1970).

'All we can say is to echo the words of Byron; if we laugh at any mortal thing it is that we may not weep.'

Tomás Mac Anna, Abbey Director, in reply to protest (16 September 1970).

'Northern Ireland is like one of her great sons, George Best – on the transfer list but no rash of offers.'

John D. Stewan (9 December 1972).

'It came together with such force it was known as the Collision Government.'

Maureen Potter, on the formation of the new Fianna Fáil Government (1973).

'I have a letter here from a West Belfast Roman Catholic. It says "Dear Dr Paisley, I think I may be homosexual, what should I do?" Well, West Belfast Roman Catholic, you should repent your evil ways because you are an abomination before the Lord. [Pause.] I don't know what you should do about your homosexuality.'

Ian Paisley character, played by the Hole in the Wall Gang.

Ma: 'I wish they'd take the UDA and the IRA and the UVF and the INLA and put them all on an island and let them shoot each other all they want.'

Emer: 'But Ma, this is an island and that's exactly what they are doing.'

Hole in the Wall Gang, *Two Ceasefires and a Wedding*.

'Everyone is now talking about peace in the North, and building a future in the North, and we're coming together and we're building this and we're building that. I don't mean to worry anyone, but the last thing we built in Belfast went down with Leonardo di Caprio and Kate Winslet hanging off the back of it.'

Patrick Kielty.

'What IRA are they talking about? There's so many of them now isn't there? There's the Real IRA, the Surreal IRA, the Continuity IRA, the Provisional IRA, the Official IRA, Low Fat IRA, Diet IRA, I Can't Believe It's Not The IRA.'

Patrick Kielty.

'The Craic We Had the Day We Died for Ireland.'

Title of song by Ding Dong Denny O'Reilly, the stage name of Paul Woodfall.

'"The army says that a bomb abandoned in Lurgan this week had a sophisticated timing device. It was set to go off just after the IRA statement but just before people start asking why the IRA hasn't decommissioned yet," explained Lt. Col. Julian Sandhurst yesterday. Nobody has been taken in by questioning.'

Newton Emerson, on the final edition of portadownnews.com (15 August 2005).

'There will be a total cessation of everything we did during our last total cessation.'

Newton Emerson, spoof IRA statement, portadownnews.com (8 August 2005).

'Ian Paisley has vowed to keep Sinn Féin out of government by keeping himself out of government. "There will be no surrender to the IRA's surrender," said the leader of Northern

Ireland's largest party yesterday. "After fifty years in politics, republicans are still as dangerous as I have always needed them to be and it is still not my fault."'

Newton Emerson, portadownnews.com (8 August 2005).

'It's important to bring the correct identification with you when you go to vote. To accommodate Portadown's social diversity, a wide range of documentation is now acceptable: Electoral Ward A: British passport, TV licence, mortgage statement, wage slip, gun licence. Electoral Ward B: Irish passport, court summons, rent arrears notice, UB40, gun.

Newton Emerson, portadownnews.com (18 May 2001).

'On my visit to Slovenia I told them how much we loved Sleveens in Ireland. In fact I told them there were a lot of Sleveens in my own party.'

'Diary of a Northside Taoiseach', *Phoenix* Magazine (2004).

Scandals

Clientelism and jobbery were so much part and parcel of politics that the politicians were surprised people got cross about it. It is only a bit of harmless fun, they told us. And then Ben Dunne was caught with a call girl in an Orlando hotel.

'Trí as anso bís do accallaim: rí imma gabáil, Gall ina lúirig, athech do muin commairchi.' ('Three that are most difficult to talk to: a king about his booty, a Viking in his hauberk, a boor who is under patronage.')

Kuno Meyer, *The Triads of Ireland* (14th century).

'Trí àta mesa do fhlaith: lén, brath, míairle.' ('Three things that are worst for a chief: sloth, treachery, evil counsel.')

Kuno Meyer, *The Triads of Ireland* (14th century).

'I have got the votes of the plain people of Baltinglass. Who were those on the protest committee? Cousins of the British queen, a gentleman from Poland, another from another part of the country and the famous Major-

General Dennis, the rackrenter and member of the Basil Brooke fifth column.'

James Everett (20 June 1951). He had appointed a supporter, Michael Farrell, to be postmaster at Baltinglass, taking the position away from Helen Cooke and her family, who had had it for generations.

'Unsavoury matters are inseparable from politics.'

Seán MacBride, Clann na Poblachta leader, giving his reaction to the Battle of Baltinglass.

'We will be told from the opposite benches that a big police force like the Civic Guards is a necessity in this country. It is, of course, a necessity, a necessity to give the hangers-on of the Cumann na nGaedhael Party jobs – to provide jobs for them.'

S.E. Holt (1 November 1928).

'It is not the policy of this party to provide jobs for its members; it may be of the government party.'

Seán MacEntee (27 February 1929).

'The introduction of this bill merely shows how well founded was my suspicion when I asked the question as to whether this bill was intended to provide jobs for the defeated candidates of the Clann na Poblachta Party.'

Gerry Boland (13 July 1949).

Charles J. Haughey: 'You know about the cargo that is coming in to Dublin airport on Sunday?'

Peter Berry: 'Yes Minister.'

Charles J. Haughey: 'Can it be let through on a guarantee

it will go direct to the North?'

Peter Berry: 'No.'

Charles J. Haughey: 'I think that is a bad decision. Does Ó Móráin know?'

Peter Berry: 'Yes.'

Charles J. Haughey: 'What will happen when it arrives?'

Peter Berry: 'It will be grabbed.'

Charles J. Haughey: 'I had better have it called off.'

Telephone conversation between Department of Justice Secretary Peter Berry and Charles J. Haughey on what would happen if arms were imported without the knowledge of the cabinet (18 April 1970).

'I have run no guns; I have procured no guns; I have paid for no guns, and I have provided money to pay for no guns.'

Neil Blaney, having resigned from government after the Arms Crisis (8 May 1970).

'Amnesty International is concerned that despite widespread allegations made public in Ireland earlier this year that persons under arrest have been maltreated, the Government of the time saw no necessity to instigate an impartial inquiry.'

Amnesty International (14 October 1977).

'I reiterate firmly and categorically that I did not attempt, nor did I mislead this House with regard to meetings with the Chairman of Greencore. As I said, taking the record as a whole, it is quite clear that what I was rebutting to Deputy Spring was any suggestion that a meeting of the kind he was talking about took place. I was saying that no meeting at which I had made an improper suggestion to the Chairman of Greencore ever took place. If one reads the record fully and takes all the combination of answers into account, a fair-minded person would not come to any other conclusion.'

Charles J. Haughey, rebutting another allegation (October 1991).

'I now categorically state that at no time have I taken part in any illegal importation or attempted importation of arms into this country.'

Charles J. Haughey (8 May 1970).

'Almost all of the dramatic scandals and revelations which rocked Irish political life from the 1990s can be traced to an anonymous fixer working for Stouffer's Resort Hotel, Orlando, Florida. It was he who provided Ben Dunne with over forty grammes of cocaine in February 1992.'

Gene Kerrigan and Pat Brennan, *This Great Little Nation: The A-Z of Irish Scandals and Controversies* (1999).

'Taxi drivers know who Mr Big is. My eight-year-old daughter knows who Mr Big is.'

Sam Smyth, journalist, on the *Gerry Ryan Radio Show*, at a time when rumours about the Ben Dunne payments were circulating (1994).

'The initial legislation was not directed at Irish writers, although the trawl it constructed managed to capture them also. The legislation was intended to keep the Irish people pure in mind and tranquil in the most sensitive areas of their anatomy. In short, it was all about Ireland's great preoccupation: the illicit "dart of the other thing", or sex as it is known in the civilised world.'

Censorship legislation, as described by Breandán Ó hEithir, *The Begrudger's Guide to Irish Politics* (1986).

'With regard to contraception, abortion and all those nonsensical things, the Minister should put his two feet on top of them – if we wanted a healthy nation this was what the Minister should be doing or considering – not the ridiculous suggestion that if you do not give up smoking you will die of cancer.'

Stephen Coughlan (25 March 1971).

Sex and its Practitioners: The Three-Letter Word

Legislating for the bedroom should be an uncomfortable business, but the politicians seemed to be happy to decide everyone else's behaviour while reserving some deviations for themselves.

'It is popular in Europe to talk of sex, divorce and drugs. These things are foreign in Ireland and to Ireland and we want them kept foreign.'

Oliver J. Flanagan (10 March 1971).

Atá dano sechtmonail i corus rig; i domnach do ol chorma, ar ní flaith techte nad ingella laith as cách ndomnach; luan do breithemnacht, do choccertad tuath; máirt oic fidchill; cetain do deicsiu milchoin oic tofunn; taradain do lanamnas; ain diden do rethaib ech; satharn do brethaib. [Sunday is for drinking ale, Monday for legal business, for the adjudication between tuath; Tuesday for chess; Wednesday for seeing greyhounds coursing; Thursday for marital intercourse; Friday for horse-racing; Saturday for judgements.]

Week in the life of an ancient Irish king, translated by T. F. Barrington, *Crith Gablach* 700AD.

'The people before us didn't rat on their children for the sake of Protestant schooling, land or soup. Surely we won't for the sake of easy sex.'

Dr Cornelius Lucey, Bishop of Cork and Ross (1 May 1971).

'The availability of contraceptives will, in my opinion, add more serious consequences to those already there. You do not quench a fire by sprinkling it with petrol.'

Oliver J. Flanagan (11 July 1974).

'I would not like to leave contraception on the long finger too long.'

Jack Lynch (23 May 1971).

'Consexual sexual intercourse.

Bertie Ahern, speaking in Dáil Éireann (June 2006).

'It should be treated as a dead letter.'

Kevin McNamara, Archbishop of Dublin, commenting on legislation to make contraceptives available to people over eighteen (21 November 1984).

'Most people are aware of my current domestic situation but they haven't yet heard of the Parnellite lives of people from the top to the bottom in Fianna Fáil.'

Charlie McCreevy (21 April 1985).

'They came into a meeting about contraceptives and kept talking about rolls and cream. At the end of it I was starving.'
Joe Bermingham (attrib.), from his time preparing family-planning legislation as junior minister in the Department of Health.

'We don't ignore the reality of condoms, but condoms in their proper place.'
Joseph Duffy, Bishop of Clogher (13 March 1990).

'The way in which [condoms] affect behaviour could also have the consequence of spreading AIDS.'
Dr Michael Smith, Bishop of Meath (11 March 1991).

'For the first time I feel I am a full citizen in my own country.'
Senator David Norris, speaking after the passing of a bill decriminalising homosexual acts (26 June 1993).

Sinn Féin

A bewildering array of secessionist parties have carried the untranslatable name of Sinn Féin, whose major shared characteristic has been the rather novel premise that it is a political party that refused to participate in parliamentary politics. The dual-monarchy party which was founded in 1904 had evolved considerably into a Republican one when it won seven famous by-elections in the aftermath of 1916 and eighty-three seats out of 104 in the 1918 election. The bit of Sinn Féin that accepted the Treaty met at the Mansion House in January 1923 and formed Cumann na nGaedhael. Sinn Féin was reorganised under Eamon de Valera until he lost a vote on abstention and departed to form Fianna Fáil in 1926. In January 1970, the Official Sinn Féin, which was to become the Workers' Party, Democratic Left and merge with Labour, were in the minority, and the Provisional Sinn Féin, loyal to abstention, withdrew. In 1987, it threw out abstention, causing another rump to found Republican Sinn Féin, which continues to do what it knows best – stay out of parliamentary politics until it gets its own way.

'Who here really believes we can win the war through the ballot box? But will anyone here object if, with a ballot paper in this hand, and an armalite in this hand, we take power in Ireland?'

Danny Morrison, Sinn Féin Director of Publicity, addressing the party Ard Fheis in Dublin (31 October 1981).

'If you walk out of this hall today the only place you are going is home. Don't go, my friends. We will lead you to the Republic.'

Martin McGuinness, Sinn Féin Vice President at the party's Ard Chomhairle, before a vote of 429 to 161 ended its abstentionist policy. Dissident members walked out to form Republican Sinn Féin (2 November 1986).

'I come here with a message of peace. We're going to have peace, not in forty or fifty years time, but in our time.'

Gerry Adams (1 February 1994).

'I am not a member of the IRA but I have in the past been involved in the defence of a community which has suffered greatly at the hands of British occupation forces.'

Martin McGuinness (3 April 1994).

'Tiocfaidh Armani.'

Parody of IRA slogan, after Gerry Adams' tour of USA (1994).

'We are the risen people.'

Martin McGuinness (8 August 1993).

'We used to think of the Provos as Fianna Fáil with guns. After the ceasefires, they became Fianna Fáil with a lingering nostalgia for things that go bang in the night. Sinn Féin has a number of radical members with working-class roots but like Fianna Fáil they can be expected to get over that.'

Gene Kerrigan, *Never Make a Promise You Can't Break: How to Succeed in Irish Politics* (2002).

'He dyed for Ireland.'

Comment after Gerry Adams' hair was mysteriously transformed from red to black.

'Tiocfaidh ár L.A.'

Parody of IRA slogan, after Gerry Adams' tour of America, which included visit to Los Angeles (1994).

'We are in an era of conflict resolution. I do think it's the end game.'

Pat Doherty (31 May 1996).

'Sinn Féin is not involved in armed struggle. Sinn Féin does not advocate armed struggle. We are truly and absolutely committed to democratic and peaceful means of resolving political problems.'

Gerry Adams (20 June 1996).

'Britain might have once ruled the waves, now it is reduced to waiving the rules.'

Gerry Adams (19 May 1997).

'Ulster Unionists talk about the need to jump together, but I cannot jump far with Mr Trimble on my back.'

Gerry Adams (June 1998).

Slogans, Posters and PPBs

Nobody in politics has ever heard of anyone changing a vote because of a slogan. But they love thinking up new and increasingly meaningless ones all the same.

'Enough of the Cowboys, Time for the Indians.'
Dr Moosajee Bhamjee, slogan in Clare constituency, during the 1992 general election campaign.

'Here comes Oliver J. There goes Oliver J.'
Sign on Oliver J. Flanagan's bicycle during his campaign as leader of the Monetary Reform Party.

'Keep Our Flag Green.'
Cumann na nGaedhael slogan (1932).

'Don't Change Horses While Crossing the Stream.'
Fianna Fáil general election slogan (1943).

'The Dev You Know Is Better than the Devil You Don't.'
Fianna Fáil slogan (1948).

'Wives: Get Your Husbands Off to Work. Vote Fianna Fáil.'
Fianna Fáil slogan (1957).

'Let Lemass Lead On.'
Fianna Fáil slogan (1965).

'The Seventies Will Be Socialist.'
Labour Party slogan (1969).

'Bring Back Jack.'
Fianna Fáil slogan (1973).

'Don't Blame Me, I Voted Fianna Fáil.'
Slogan produced by Fianna Fáil after the 1981 election.

'There Is a Better Way.'
Fianna Fáil slogan (1987).

'Health Cuts Hurt the Old, the Poor and the Handicapped.'
Fianna Fáil slogan (1987), to which a graffiti artist added 'promises, promises'.

'Much Done, More to Do.'
Fianna Fáil slogan (2002).

'A Breath of Fresh Air.'
Proinsias De Rossa, slogan for the European election (1989).

'A Vote for Ireland a Nation, a Vote Against Conscription, a Vote Against Partition, a Vote for Ireland's Language, and for Ireland's Ideals and Civilisation.'

Sinn Féin slogan in the Clare by-election (1917).

'We'll Give You the Cage but You'll Have to Find the Bird Yourself.'

Slogan of Ger Connolly TD, Fianna Fáil, after a change in the law under which single people qualified for housing grants.

'You Are Now Entering Free Derry.'

Slogan on a gable wall of a house on the Lecky Road in Derry painted by Liam Hillen (5 January 1969). It was based on the inscription outside Berkeley College 'You are now entering free Berkeley', the expression of the Berkely Free Speech Movement led by Lenny Claser and others. It was later mistakenly attributed to John "Caker" Casey. It became an iconic symbol of the Troubles and a tourist attraction.

'Down with this sort of thing!'

Protest placard carried by Fr Ted Crilly (Dermot Morgan) in the television series *Father Ted*, scripted by Arthur Mathews and Graham Linehan (1995-8).

'Careful Now!'

Placard carried by Fr Dougal McGuire, responding to 'Down with this sort of thing!' in the television series *Father Ted*, scripted by Arthur Mathews and Graham Linehan (1995-8).

'Open with a series of short sharply edited images. No shot must last longer than four seconds. At least four-fifths of the footage you use will have nothing to do with politics or politicians.

An example of the kind of sequence you need is: a plane taking off, waves crashing on a beach, a machine ploughing a field with a rainbow in the background, the party leader laughing, a lifeboat being launched (symbolises the heroic party coming to the rescue of the nation, a goal being scored at an All-Ireland final, the crowd rising to its feet cheering, waving arms, the party leader nodding thoughtfully talking to a pensioner, a lollipop lady helping kids across the road, a candidate shaking hands on a voter's doorstep, a field of wheat gently waving in the sun, that kind of thing – positive, energetic, concerned and capable.'

Gene Kerrigan, *Never Make a Promise You Can't Break: How to Succeed in Irish Politics* (2002).

'Single-Party Government. No Thanks!'

Michael McDowell, personal election slogan (2002).

'We Do Not Care What Shirt You Wore.'

Clann na Poblachta slogan for general election (1948).

'Vote Dev and Yes.'

Slogan for presidential election and referendum abolishing proportional representation (1959). Dev won, but the people voted no to changing from proportional representation.

'England's difficulty is Ireland's opportunity.'

Slogan of the National Volunteers (1916).

Soldiers

While politicians for all their faults are generally interested in making things better, military men are generally interested only in making things worse. They will say that is to make things better in the longer term, but they would say that, wouldn't they?

'Now for our Irish wars: / We must supplant these rough rug-headed kerns, / Which live like venom where no venom else / But only they have privilege to live.'

William Shakespeare, *Richard II.*

'Let England fight her own battles – we have done so long enough.'

Bulmer Hobson in an anti-enlistment leaflet (1905).

'It has pleased God to bless our endeavours at Drogheda . . . I believe we put to the sword the whole number of the defendants. I do not think thirty of the whole number escaped with their lives. Those that did, are in safe custody for the Barbados . . . I wish that all honest hearts may give the glory of this to God alone, to whom indeed the praise of this mercy belongs.'

Oliver Cromwell, in a letter to the Hon. John Bradshaw, President of the Council of State (September 1649).

'Nor law, nor duty bade me fight, / Nor public man, nor angry crowds, / A lonely impulse of delight / Drove to this tumult in the clouds; / I balanced all, brought all to mind, / The years to come seemed waste of breath, / A waste of breath the years behind / In balance with this life, this death.'

W.B. Yeats, 'An Irish Airman Foresees his Death', in *The Wild Swans at Coole and Other Poems* (1919).

'As long as war is regarded as wicked, it will always have its fascination. When it is looked upon as vulgar, it will cease to be popular.'

Oscar Wilde, 'The Critic as Artist'.

'Now if you go to the fighting line and there to fight the Boer, / Will you kindly hould the Dublins back, and let the culchies go before.'

Anonymous, 'Get Me Down My Petticoat', street ballad.

'The Dublin worker is not a natural revolutionary, but he is a natural soldier.'

Thomas Kettle, *Labour and Civilisation*.

'The English always have their wars in someone else's country.'

Brendan Behan, quoted in Sean McCann, *The Wit of Brendan Behan* (1968).

'If I live, I mean to spend the rest of my life working for perpetual peace. I have seen war and faced artillery and know what an outrage it is against simple men.'

Thomas Kettle, *Poems and Parodies*.

'They proceeded to strike, mangle, slaughter and cut down one another for a long time, so that men were soon laid low, heroes wounded, youths slain and robust heroes mangled in the slaughter.'

Annals of the Four Masters (1567).

'The organisation of the north being thus deranged, the colonels flinched and the chief of the Antrim men Robert Simms not appearing, the duty fell on Henry J. McCracken.'

James Hope (attrib.), United Irish Leader.

'King James had behind him the letter of the law just as completely as Mr Asquith . . . the King had the largest army which had ever been seen in England. What happened? There was no civil war. There was a revolution, and the King disappeared. Why? Because his own army refused to fight for him.'

Andrew Bonar Law, British Conservative leader, in a Dublin speech regarded as an incitement to the british army to mutiny if ordered to move against Ulster Unionists (28 November 1913).

'The British officer seldom likes Irish soldiers; but he always tries to have a certain proportion of them in his battalion, because, partly from a want of common sense which leads them to value their lives less than Englishmen do (lives are really less worth living in a poor country), and partly because even the most cowardly Irishman feels obliged to outdo an Englishman in bravery if possible, and at least to set a pilous pace for him, Irish soldiers give impetus to those military operations which require for their spirited execution more devilment than prudence.'

George Bernard Shaw, preface to *O'Flaherty VC* (1919).

'Oh Irishmen, dear countrymen, take heed of what we say, for if you do England's dirty work, you will surely rue the day.'

James Larkin (25 July 1914).

'Should a German army land in Ireland tomorrow, we should be perfectly justified in joining it, if by doing so we could rid this country once and for all from its connection with the Brigand Empire that drags us unwillingly to war.'

James Connolly (1 August 1914).

'Give me 5,000 men and I will say thank you. Give me 10,000 and I will take off my hat to you.'

Lord Kitchener, to John Redmond (7 August 1914).

'The more genuine and successful the local volunteer movement in Ulster becomes, the more completely does it establish the principle that Irishmen have the right to decide and govern their own national affairs.'

Eoin MacNeill, speaking at the foundation meeting of Irish Volunteers (25 November 1913).

'I wish it then to be clearly understood that under present conditions I am definitely opposed to any proposal that may come forward involving insurrection. I am certain that the only possible basis for successful revolutionary action is deep and widespread popular discontent. We have only to look around us in the streets to realise that no such condition exists in Ireland.'

Eoin MacNeill, in a memorandum to the Irish Volunteers (February 1916).

'Owing to the very critical position, all orders given to Irish Volunteers for tomorrow, Easter Sunday, are hereby rescinded, and no parades, marches or other movements of Irish Volunteers will take place.'

Eoin MacNeill, *Sunday Independent* (23 April 1916).

'The four City Battalions will parade for inspection and route march at 10 a.m. today.'

Notice by Thomas MacDonagh, countersigned by Padraig Pearse, signalling start of The Easter Rising (24 April 1916).

'The Irish ought to be grateful to us. With a minimum of casualties to the civilian population, we have succeeded in removing some third-rate poets.'

Captain David Platt, British officer, in letter to his wife Jane in the aftermath of The Easter Rising (20 May 1916). Quoted in Declan Kiberd, *Inventing Ireland* (1995).

'Many would like to do with the British what we read that Brian Boru did with the Danes, not far from here. But we did not do it. We were not able to do it.'

Kevin O'Higgins, speaking in Dáil Éireann (18 September 1922).

'Men are standing in the path today, armed men, saying to the masked men of this nation, you must not take a certain course. That is a position which never has been conceded here. Some men must be allowed to work that Treaty settlement.'

Kevin O'Higgins, speaking in Dáil Éireann on the re-establishment of civic administration (29 September 1922).

'Now the life of this nation and the honour of this nation is worth the lives of many individuals. And we, in grave consultation and in grave council, have decided that if it is necessary to take the lives of many individuals then the lives of many individuals will be taken.'

Kevin O'Higgins, speaking in Dáil Éireann in defence of military executions (17 November 1922).

'Unless we take very stern measures, we will not throw back the tide of lawlessness and the tide of lust and loot that some mad political leaders have stirred up in their train in this country.'

General Richard Mulcahy, speaking in Dáil Éireann in defence of military executions (17 November 1922).

'Two army officers have attempted to involve the Army in a challenge to the authority of the Government. This is an outrageous departure from the spirit of the Army. It will not be tolerated.'

General Richard Mulcahy (10 March 1924).

'We are not equipped to face even a minimum attack from outside. We haven't the ships, the planes, the artillery, the Armour . . . Sovereignty is the ability to defend ourselves or to be defended. The twenty-six-county state would do well to grow to such mature sovereignty before we think about other areas of sovereignty like Northern Ireland.'

Lieutenant-General Carl O'Sullivan (2 February 1982).

'We recognise that a military commitment will be an inevitable consequence of our joining the Common Market and ultimately we would be prepared to yield even the technical label of our neutrality.'

Seán Lemass (June 1962).

'The attempt by army officers to challenge the Government is a challenge to the democratic foundations of the State, to the very basis of parliamentary representation and of responsible government.'

William T. Cosgrave (11 March 1924).

'Whenever I see a hen sitting for two years on an egg I know that the egg is addled, and whenever I see a minister sitting for two years on a bill, I have a very strong suspicion that the same will be the case.'

Major Bryan Cooper, speaking in Dáil Éireann on Army Pensions (No. 2) Bill 1926, Dáil Éireann (25 January 1927).

'If they [the British] may use their tanks and steel-armoured cars, why should we hesitate to use stone walls and ditches? Why should the use of the element of surprise be denied to us?'

Eamon de Valera (30 March 1921). Quoted in Dorothy Macardle, *The Irish Republic* (1951).

'The over-rider of the people's rights.'

General Richard Mulcahy, describing himself (26 June 1924).

'When you came to this land / You said you came to understand / Soldier, we are tired of your understanding. / Tired of British troops on Irish soil / Tired of the knock upon the door / Tired of the rifle butt on the head / Tired of the jails, the gas, the beatings / Tired of the deaths of our friends / Tired of the tears and the funerals / Those endless endless, funerals. / Is this your understanding?'

Patrick Galvin, *Letter to a British Soldier on Irish Soil* (1972).

'A general and a bit of shooting makes you forget your troubles . . . it takes your mind off the cost of living.'

Brendan Behan, *The Hostage* (1958).

'Christ, I'm in the wrong house.'

Official IRA gunman, after shooting dead Belfast man Owen McVeigh in front of his family during a Republican feud (11 November 1975).

'When I came back to Dublin, I was court-martialed in my absence and sentenced to death in my absence, so I said they could shoot me in my absence.'

Brendan Behan, *The Hostage* (1958).

'They who ruled the seven seas now blow up bridges at Crossmaglen and lesser places little marked on maps.'

Benedict Kiely, *All the Way to Bantry Bay and Other Irish Journeys* (1978).

Songs, Rhymes
and Troubadours

From the 'Shan Van Vocht' to 'The Fields of Athenry', some of Ireland's most oft-sung songs have had a political edge. As Dublin balladeer Frank Harte used to say 'those in power write the history – those who suffer write the songs.' It probably explains the speed at which politicals songs entered popular culture. Most spectacularly, T.D. Sullivan's 'God Save Ireland' was being sung through the land within days of its appearence in *The Nation* newspaper in December 1867 and within three weeks of the execution of the rebels it was immortalised. And with political songs so prevalent at Ireland's fair and public houses, it was inevitable that as the age dawned of vinyl records, CDs and digital music files, clever political satire would eventually leave the more serious stuff behind.

'I'm very glad you asked me that for at this point in time / In the circumstances that prevail there is in the pipeline / Infrastructural implications interfaced with lines of thought /

Which lead to grassroots viabilities / Which at this point I'd rather not / Enunciate in ambiguities but rather seek to find / Negotiated compromises which are the bottom line / Which with full and frank discussions which seek to integrate / With fundamental principles to which we all relate / Not in doctrinaire philosophy which any fool can see / But inescapable hypothesis confronting you and me / In the interests of the common good well you need never fear / For I have the matter well in hand I'm glad I made things clear.'

Mickey McConnell, former Irish journalist and ballad-writer, 'The Politicians' Song', parodying political jargon (1992).

'Ho, Brother Teague, dost hear the Decree? / Lilli Burlero Bullen a-la / That we shall have a new Deputy / Lilli Burlero Bullena-la.'

Thomas Wharton, 'A New Song', based on the Jacobite cry 'An Lile ba Leir-oh, buileann an la.' The music now serves as the theme for the BBC World Service (1688).

'I am no Rogue, no Ribbonman, / No Croppy, Whig, or Tory oh; / I'm guilty not of any crime / Of petty or high thraison, oh.'

Jeremiah O'Ryan, 'The Peeler and the Goat'.

'And soon the bright Orange put down the Green Rag, / Down, down, Croppies lie down.'

'Croppies Lie Down', Orange ballad.

'Almost all the Irish political songs are too desponding or weak to content a people marching to independence as proudly as if they never had been slaves.'

Thomas Davis, 'Our Music and Poetry'.

'And then I prayed I yet might see / Our fetters rent in twain, / And Ireland, long a province, be / A nation once again.'

Thomas Davis, 'A Nation Once Again'.

'But – hark! – some voice like thunder spake, / "The West's awake, the West's awake" / Sing oh! hurrah! let England quake, / We'll watch till death for Erin's sake!'

Thomas Davis, 'The West's Awake'.

'Whether on the scaffold high, or in battlefield we die, / Oh what matter, when for Erin dear we fall!'

T.D. Sullivan, 'God Save Ireland'.

'Long years that green and lovely vale / Has nursed Parnell her grandest Gael / And curse the land that has betrayed / Fair Avondale's proud eagle.'

Song by Parnellite supporters (1891).

'Come tenant farmers rally round, / Make your cheers the air resound / For Charles Stewart Parnell sound / The friend of Paddy's nation.'

Broadside on death of Charles Stewart Parnell (1891).

'In Mountjoy Jail one Monday morning, / High upon the gallows tree, / Kevin Barry gave his young life / For the cause of liberty.'

'Kevin Barry', first collected in Carl Sandburg's American Songbag (1927). The song was written by one of three claimed authors, an anonymous Irishman in Glasgow who published it as a broadside, Terrence Ward later of the *Irish Press* and Peter Ellis of Crydon Park, Marino in Dublin, who composed it on the evening of Kevin Barry's execution 1 November 1920 and it was given to Christy Russell to sing. The tune was already popular as 'Rolling Home Across the Sea'. The song was an instant success and gained international recognition when recorded by Paul Robeson.

'I thought Kevin Barry was shot.'
Desmond O'Malley (1970).

'Another martyr for old Ireland / Another murder for the crown / Whose brutal laws may kill the Irish / But can't keep their spirit down.'
'Kevin Barry'.

'We defeated Conscription in spite of their threats, / And we're going to defeat old Lloyd-George and his pets; / For Ireland and Freedom we're here to a man, / And we'll humble the pride of the bold Black and Tan.'
'The Bold Black and Tan'.

'I went to see David, to London to David, / I went to see David and what did he do? / He gave me a Free State, a nice little Free State, / A Free State that's tied up with Red, White and Blue.'
'The Irish Free State'.

'We are still tryin' to reach the future through the past, still tryin' to carve tomorrow through a tombstone.'
Paul Brady, 'The Island' (1986).

'There were Bren guns and Sten guns and Whippet tanks galore. / And the battle raging up and down from pub to general store. / Between the vintner and the cook the pot

was quite upset, / And the Minister swore this Irish stew
was the worst he'd ever ate.'

'The Battle of Baltinglass', a parody based on the argument
over whether the running of the post office in Baltinglass
was awarded to a political favourite (1953).

'Legion of the Rearguard, answering Ireland's call, / Hark their
martial tramp is heard from Cork to Donegal, / Tone and
Emmett guide you, though your task be hard, / De Valera
lead you! Soldiers of the Legion of the Rearguard.'

P.J. Sheehy, de Valera supporter, who wrote the Fianna Fáil
party anthem while interned in the Curragh (1922).

'A tinker and / A tailor and / An IRA; / An Auxie man / A
Black-and-Tan / A thief.'

Dublin children's rhyme, quoted in Leslie Daiken, *Out Goes
She*, a compilation of Dublin street rhymes.

'Eeeny Meeney Maximoe, / Catch James Dillon by the toe, /
If he screams OLIVER, let him go, / Eeeny Meeny Maximoe.'

Rhyme referring to Locke's Distillery scandal of 1947, when
criminal Alexander Maximoe and his associates attempted to
acquire the whiskey stock in Kilbeggan for sale on the black
market, quoted by Breandán Ó hEithir, *The Begrudger's
Guide to Irish Politics* (1986).

'I dreamt that Mr Haughey had recaptured Crossmaglen, /
Then Garret got re-elected and he gave it back again. / Dick
Spring and Roger Casement were on board the Marita Ann
/ And as she sailed into Fenit they were singing 'Banna
Strand'. / I dreamt Archbishop MacNamara was on Spike
Island for three nights, / Having been arrested for supporting

travellers' rights. / I dreamt that Ruairi Quinn was smoking marijuana in the Dáil, / Barry Desmond was handing frenchies out to scuts in Fianna Fáil . . . I dreamt of Nell McCafferty and Mary Kenny too. / The things that we got up to, but I'm not going to tell you. / I dreamt I was in a jacuzzi along with Alice Glenn, / Then I knew I'd never ever ever drink again.'

Christy Moore, 'Delirium Tremens' (1985).

'To ask the Minister for Posts and Telegraphs if he is aware that during a sponsored broadcast on 24th April a song was recited containing an insulting reference to the former Minister; and, if so, what steps he proposes to take in the matter.'

Oliver J. Flanagan (20 May 1953).

'Deputy Flanagan thinks that I am idiotic enough to spend my time looking for records in Radio Éireann in which to criticise the Opposition. That suggestion is so ludicrous as not to be worthy of consideration.'

Erskine Childers, in reply to the criticism by Oliver J.
Flanagan of the broadcast of a satirical song about the Battle of Baltinglass on Radio Éireann (20 May 1953).

'Armoured cars and tanks and guns, / Came to take away our sons, / But every man will stand behind / The men behind the wire.'

Paddy McGuigan, 'The Men Behind the Wire' (September 1971).

'I have four green fields, one of them's in bondage.'

Tommy Makem, 'Four Green Fields' (1972).

'With their tanks and their guns, / Oh my God what have
they done / To the town I loved so well?'
Phil Coulter, 'The Town I Loved So Well' (1976).

'Don't cry for me, Ballymena.'
Roy Mason, Secretary of State for Northern Ireland. Words
he was singing as he took off in his helicopter from
Stormont Castle (3 May 1977).

'Everybody needs a break / Climb a mountain or jump in a
lake / Seán Doherty goes to the Rose of Tralee / And Oliver
J. Flanagan goes swimming in the Holy Sea.'
Christy Moore, 'Lisdoonvaarna', a 500-word, four-and-a-half-
minute musing on life in Ireland, including the scandal the
crashing of Justice Minister Seán Doherty's state car at the
Rose of Tralee festival in 1982 (1984).

'She keeps fools for counsel, / She keeps the wig and gown,
/ The cloth and the bloody warfare, / The stars and the
stripes and crown, / Still we pray for a better day now, / God
willing it's for the best, / I've just seen the harp on the penny
/ With the dollar on her naked breast.'
Jimmy MacCarthy, 'Mystic Lipstick' (1989).

'Oh my darling Clementine.'
Peter Brooke, Secretary of State for Northern Ireland, singing
on *The Late Late Show,* his performance subsequently led to
his resignation (17 January 1992).

'I imagine that singing that song will give a fair amount of
ammunition to a fair number of people.'
Gay Byrne (17 January 1992).

'I think the sad epitaph of this rainbow government will be: Here lies the rainbow, red, white and blue, which worked for itself but never for you.'

Bertie Ahern attempting some poetry as the Dáil is dissolved (1997).

'In a matter of seconds confusion did reign / The room was in darkness, fire exits were chained.'

Christy Moore, 'They Never Came Home', song about the Stardust disaster in Artane (9 August 1985).

'Hold the tide with pitchfork and with shovel; / Stop the restiveness that's bitin' at the people. / Shirts go chasin' backwards up the ceilin', / And licences are comin' home to roost. / Call the guards, and bid them snaffle Blythe / Blythe's a bally gunman in disguise. . . . Duffy too! he's dangerous at large. . . . Clap the pair of 'em in clink this very night! [Chorus:] Woe's the day! My head is gone astray! / Ev'rything is blue! I think I have the flu! / Blue Shirts light around my bed at night. / And at dawn they dance a fling in Leinster Lawn!'

Song from the *Blueshirt* magazine (October 1932).

Spin Doctors

Anyone who thinks spin-doctoring is new should look at the genealogy lists of the medieval kings and the squabble for place-legend in the dindsenchas. It could be that the very earliest piece of prose in the Irish language was a piece of spin.

'Una duce, una voce.'

P.J. Mara, remarking on how the Fianna Fáil party had 'one leader, one voice', after party whip was removed from Desmond O'Malley (26 May 1984). Mara said it was intended as much a send-up of Haughey as it was a put-down of Fianna Fáil dissidents. He added, 'There will be no more nibbling at my leader's bum.' It was regarded as off the record by the journalists present but was then quoted by Geraldine Kennedy in the *Sunday Press*.

'You go into that room where they all hate me and you give them this.'

Charles J. Haughey, to P.J. Mara after publication of the 'una duce, una voce' remark.

'Cudillo, el Diablo.'

P.J. Mara, references to Charles J. Haughey in months after 'Una duce, una voce' remark.

'I want none of that old arms trial shite.'

P.J. Mara, giving his prerequisite for media interviews in the 1980s.

'If Charles Haughey had listened to P.J. Mara more often he would have been more successful.'

Charlie McCreevy, on P.J. Mara, quoted by Tim Ryan, *P.J. Mara* (1992).

'Renowned for colourful language and denials, he manages to keep reporters on side by wit, impudence and telling them to fuck off, which they love.'

Liam Collins, on P.J. Mara, *Sunday Independent.*

'Mara, you've finally blown it. I'm ruined.'

Charles J. Haughey reacting to the publication of an expletive-laden interview with John Waters in *Hot Press* (29 November 1984). Quoted by Tim Ryan, *P.J. Mara* (1992).

P.J. Mara: 'Here is the cup of tea you asked for, Boss.'

Charles J. Haughey: 'Cup of tea?'

P.J. Mara: 'You asked me to get you a cup of tea.'

Charles J. Haughey: 'For God's sake, Mara, I never—'

P.J. Mara: 'I wrote it down, Boss.'

Charles J. Haughey: 'I never attempted to mislead you on the issue of the cup of tea. It is true I started to say cup of tea, but I was interrupted in mid-sentence. Had I not been, I would have told you that what I wanted was a cup of tea as has no chockie bickie with it.'

Sketch on satirical radio programme *Scrap Saturday*, scripted by Owen Roe, Gerry Stembridge and Dermot Morgan (1991).

'Understand the importance of a preposition. Take the word "for" below. There is a difference between "A President of All the People" and "A President for All the People." The difference is that the first one is Dublin 4 and do-gooding and the second is democratic.'

Eoghan Harris, campaign advice document to Mary Robinson (6 April 1990). Quoted in Emily O'Reilly, *Candidate: The Truth Behind the Presidential Campaign* (1991).

'From first to last you must set out to enjoy the campaign and be seen to enjoy it.'

Eoghan Harris, campaign advice document to Mary Robinson (6 April 1990). Quoted in Emily O'Reilly, *Candidate: The Truth Behind the Presidential Campaign* (1991).

'I have learned one lesson through my life, that no one is ever really close to a Taoiseach or a Prime Minister or a President.'

P.J. Mara, quoted in *The Irish Times* (27 May 2002).

'Maaaara. Yes Boss, the greatest Leader, Man of Destiny, Statesman, Titan, a Colossus.'

Scrap Saturday caricature of Haughey–P.J. Mara relationship.

'Being described as a "spin doctor" never bothered me. So, when a Co. Donegal Fianna Fáil cumann presented the Taoiseach with a magnificent old spinning wheel, I commandeered it for my office. It served rather like worry beads as I absently pumped the foot pedal up and down through endless phone conversations – merrily, cheerily, noiselessly spinning.'

Seán Duignan, *One Spin on the Merry-Go-Round* (1995).

'Custard's last stand.'

Terry Prone on the pie thrown in Michael Noonan's face during general election campaign (2 May 2002).

'Television may well have introduced the pleasures of sex to Ireland as Oliver J. Flanagan discovered, but it took an awful lot of excitement out of electioneering, the heckler in the crowd was replaced by the creepy-crawly National Handler with the syrupy slogan.'

Breandán Ó hEithir, *The Begrudger's Guide to Irish Politics* (1986).

Trade Unions

Largely apolitical in the early days, the Irish trade-union movement, which had split into Larkin and O'Brien camps in the 1920s, struggled to find unity for decades afterwards. Today, the spats are between the Congress of Trade Union and the employers' organisation, the Irish Business and Employers Confederation (IBEC).

'The great appear great only because we are on our knees.'
James Larkin.

'Whenever the workers challenged the interests of capital they found themselves confronted by the fact that the employers had influence in making the laws while they had none. New restrictions, new penal laws, more barbarous and absurd than the preceding, are enacted; the producers take measures to defeat these iniquitous laws; they endeavour by a counterforce to make head against the violences instituted against them; they resort to plots and combinations of violence to defeat the power which seeks under the name of law to repress for ever their spirit, and with it their industry. They endeavour by unjust violence towards their own number and sullen threats against their employers to keep down the depressing competition of low wages. Thus is a community converted into a theatre of war: hostile camps of the employers and labourers are everywhere formed.'

William Thompson, *An Inquiry into the Principles of the Distribution of Wealth most Conducive to Human Happiness* (1824).

'It is now war to the knife.'

Alex Boyd, Belfast trade-union leader, during the dock strike (26 June 1907).

'Although St Patrick was credited with banishing the snakes, there was one he forgot and that was Gallagher – a man who valued neither country, God nor creed.'

James Larkin, quoted in *Northern Whig*, about Thomas Gallagher of Gallagher's Tobacco during industrial dispute (18 May 1907).

'It was a scandalous thing that they should disgrace a broken bottle by using it on an officer of the British Army.'

James Larkin, after troops were brought into Belfast to break the dock strike.

'Not as Catholics or Protestants, as Nationalists or Unionists, but as Belfastmen and workers, stand together and don't be misled by the employers' game of dividing Catholic and Protestant.'

James Larkin (12 August 1907).

'In a room in a tenement in Townsend Street, with a candle in a bottle for a torch, and a billycan of tea, with a few buns for a banquet, the Church militant here on earth, called the Irish Transport and General Workers' Union, was founded.'

Seán O'Casey (4 January 1909).

'I would think there is talent enough amongst the men in the [tramways] service to form a union of their own, without allying themselves to a disreputable organisation, and placing themselves under the feet of an unscrupulous man who claims the right to give you the word of command and to issue his orders to you and to use you as tools to make him the labour dictator of Dublin.'

William Martin Murphy (19 July 1913).

'William Murphy is a humane man, known for his personal honour and charity; a "good employer" as it is called, a successful captain of enterprise, an insensitive imagination, in short, a very dangerous opponent. Picturesque, eloquent, prophetic, at once dictatorial and intimate, he [James Larkin] was, as he might say himself, the very man for the job.'

Thomas Kettle, *Labour and Civilisation.*

'I don't think I can stand Larkin as a boss much longer . . . He is consumed with jealousy and hatred of anyone who will not cringe to him and beslaver all over him.'

James Connolly (29 July 1913).

'We are going to make this a year to be spoken of in the days to come [. . .] There is a great dawn for Ireland.'

James Larkin (May 1913).

'This is not a strike, it is a lock-out of the men who have been tyrannically treated by a most unscrupulous scoundrel. We are fighting for bread and butter. By the living God, if they want war, they can have it.'

James Larkin (26 August 1913).

'I am going to O'Connell Street on Sunday. I am going there alive or dead, and I depend on you to carry me out if I'm dead.'

James Larkin, speaking at the burning of a police notice banning a meeting at Liberty Hall (29 August 1913).

'We are determined that Christ will not be crucified in Dublin by these men . . . My suggestion to the employers is that if they want peace we are prepared to meet them, but if they want war then war they will have it.'

James Larkin (4 October 1913).

'Oh, we hate the cruel tiger / And hyena and jackal / But the false and dirty blackleg / Is the vilest beast of all.'

James Connell, broadside, published during the Dublin transport strike (1913).

'I am going to talk sedition. The next time we are out for a march I want to be accompanied by four battalions of trained men with their corporals and sergeants. Why should we not drill and train men as they are doing in Ulster?'

James Connolly (13 November 1913).

'We are beaten. We make no bones about it; but we are not too badly beaten still to fight.'

James Larkin (30 January 1914).

'When the employers sacrifice one victim, the Trade Unions go one better by sacrificing a hundred.'
Seán O'Casey, *Juno and the Paycock* (1924).

'Some unions have so small a membership that the description trade union is a gross abuse of the term.'
ICTU General President (1964).

'What entered into your head to write that book, such a terrible schemozzle you caused, I couldn't take you back after that. There would be an uproar if I did.'
INTO official, representing John McGahern when he was dismissed from his teaching post for writing *The Dark*, which was banned by the Irish Censorship Board (1966).

'We demand a revision of the tax system to ease the intolerable burden on the working class so that all would pay their fair share.'
Demand by 150,000 PAYE tax protesters in Dublin and 40,000 in Cork (30 March 1979).

'Most disagreements and problems in this country come about because management wants to do something and workers are suspicious about what they want to do and why they want to do it.'
Bertie Ahern (1992).

'An ATM machine.'
Senator Joe O'Toole, on benchmarking (2002).

'I charge the Dublin Nationalist newspapers with deliberately arousing religious passion to break up the organisation of the working man, with appealing to mob law day by day . . . And I charge the Unionist press of Dublin and those who directed the police with conniving in this conspiracy.'

W.B. Yeats, letter to the *Irish Worker* during Dublin lockout (November 1913).

'Irish teachers would be forced to deliver the kind of productivity favoured by the Toyota plant in Nagasaki.'

ASTI members, opting out of benchmarking agreement (2002).

'Wake up, ASTI members. Get your elected union representatives and also your full-time union officials to do what most of you want them to do, viz., to negotiate a proper professional salary through the only mechanism currently available, benchmarking.'

Pierce Purcell, ASTI President (29 January 2002).

'When I was a child in school I carved my name on a desk and got thumped around the place by the teacher for it so don't talk to me about benchmarking.'

Letter writer in the *Sunday Independent* (7 July 2002).

Television

It took a decade of argument over cost and control before we got a home-based television station and boy, were they worried when it came that the world as we knew it would come tumbling down. They were right.

'. . . . in districts along the east coast television broadcasts are being received from another country and whether, in view of the cumulative damaging effect which these broadcasts may have on our national culture, he will take the necessary steps to introduce television broadcasting in the Republic of Ireland with a minimum of delay.'
James Everett (31 January 1952).

'Mouth-organ players from communist countries.'
James Everett, Minister for Posts and Telegraphs 1948–51, on recruits to the RTÉ Symphony Orchestra.

'It is extraordinary to find so little appreciation of the Government's desire for economy. It would be ridiculous to think of a television service in a country which has maintained no interest in it and whose people would probably be opposed to the spending of considerable sums of public money on such a luxury. Television is a long way off here.'

Department of Finance memo (1953). Quoted in Robert J. Savage, *Irish Television: The Political and Social Origins* (1996).

'The government is against the introduction of a luxury service such as television which is known to be so costly.'

Gerry Sweetman, Minister for Finance (1956). Quoted in Robert J. Savage, *Irish Television: The Political and Social Origins* (1996).

'His Holiness felt that by reason of its geographical situation, the Irish television could be of great service to the Christian religion I provided that a transmitter be installed which would be sufficiently powerful to transmit its programmes to trans-oceanic territories.'

Andrea Maria Deksur, Vatican official (21 July 1958).

'Television has come into being under a minister who refused to be stampeded into the final betrayal of Kathleen Ni Houlihan so that she was in danger of becoming Cathode Ni Houlihan.'

Eamonn Andrews, First Chairman of The RTÉ Authority, launching Teilifís Éireann at a ceremony in the Shelbourne Hotel, Dublin (31 December 1961).

'I must admit that sometimes when I think of television and radio and their immense power I feel somewhat afraid.

Like atomic energy it can be used for incalculable good but it can also do irreparable harm. While it is probably true that television is not essential to our national life, it is nevertheless an invention of enormous potentiality for good as well as evil and, if we could afford on financial grounds to have it, the proper course would be to take the invention and exploit it, under proper control.'

Eamon de Valera, on the opening night of Telefís Éireann (31 December 1961).

'On this New Year's morning I ask all of you to join with me in praying that God may abundantly bless Telefís Éireann, may the Holy Spirit guide the directors in their work, so that this new and important venture in our national life may become an asset and an ornament to our country.'

Cardinal Dalton, on the opening night of RTÉ (31 December 1961).

'I am absolutely furious about this. This protest has to be made in the fairness to Christian morality. I am referring to certain morally – or rather immorally – suggestive parts of the show which were completely unworthy of Irish television, unworthy of Irish producers, unworthy of Irish audiences.'

Thomas Ryan, Bishop of Clonfert, protesting that a participant on *The Late Late Show*, Eileen Fox, who had been asked what the colour of her nightie was on her wedding night and replied she couldn't remember, then said 'none' (12 February 1966).

'I understand that part of the entertainment offered to viewers of *The Late Late Show* on Saturday night consisted of questioning a husband and wife, in the absence of each other, about the colour of the nightdress worn by the lady on her honeymoon . . . In many homes, such a discussion is not usually engaged in, and to have it thrust into the middle of family and friends can, to some of us at all events, appear to be in utter bad taste.'

Stephen Barrett TD, Fianna Fáil (16 February 1966).

'I don't blame the people, I would rather blame the Bishop of Galway [who is a] moron.'

Brian Trevaskis, as panelist on *The Late Late Show*, remarking critically about the new Galway Cathedral, which provoked widespread objections (March 1966).

'Sex never came to Ireland until Telifís Éireann went on the air.'

Oliver J. Flanagan (1 March 1966).

'Raidio Telifís Éireann was set up by legislation as an instrument of public policy and as such is responsible to the Government.'

Seán Lemass (12 October 1966).

'RTÉ is a semi-state body, and if they sent a team to Vietnam, it would not be believed that they had done this without the approval of the Government. For a camera team it would be a conducted tour.'

Frank Aiken, Minister for External Affairs, explaining his ban on RTÉ sending a film crew to North Vietnam during the Vietnam War (13 April 1967).

'The public at large have reacted against the type of political commentators we are enduring at the moment. This sort of

cheap, blatant career-building at the expense of the public and the person whom they are interviewing is bad for the image of television. This rapid asking of questions and the shyster lawyer manner which they adopt and which one normally associates with second-rate films from America is not good enough for a national television service.'
Patrick Norton (6 March 1969).

'[RTÉ should] refrain from broadcasting any matter calculated to promote the aims or activities of any organisation which engages in, promotes, encourages or advocates the attaining of any political objective by violent means.'
Section 31 of Broadcasting Act, banning interviews on Irish radio or television with the IRA or Sinn Féin (1 October 1971).

'Mr Seán Mac Stíofáin said, "We believe that by armed struggle alone can we achieve our objectives."'
Kevin O'Kelly, RTÉ interviewer, broadcasting account of conversation with IRA leader Mac Stíofáin, for which he was jailed and RTÉ Authority dismissed for breaching Section 31 of the Broadcasting Act (19 November 1972).

'The only country where the news begins at 6.01.'
David Trimble, Ulster Unionist Party leader, criticising the broadcasting of the Angelus on RTÉ television and radio.

'Ministers should hold a middle way between extremes of aloofness and unapproachability on the one hand and over-exposure on the other, the Minister to be seen and heard when he is doing something or has something concrete to say, and not when he can only deal in vague generalities.

They should avoid participation in panel discussions on radio and television. Opposition protagonists necessarily have the advantage over Ministers, as they are cramped neither by departmental responsibility, nor by collective Cabinet responsibility, nor official secrecy.'

Conor Cruise O'Brien, in a memo to colleagues in the 1973 Coalition Government (March 1973).

"Deputies will also be interested to know that arrangements are in hand to have the Angelus Bell rung over the air each evening at 6 o'clock. It will be taken from the Pro-Cathedral in Dublin.'

James Everett, Minister for Posts and Telegraphs, announcing the Angelus would be introduced for the Holy Year 1950 (25 May 1950).

'Are we prepared, as a Christian and Catholic nation, to go the whole way and have the Rosary said over the radio in addition to hearing the bells of the Angelus? Surely that is not too much to ask in this country. Surely we have nothing to be ashamed of in regard to the heritage that is ours.'

Daniel Desmond (10 November 1953).

'[Broadcasting the Angelus on RTÉ] was essentially for Catholics and excluded a section of the population . . . if people south of the Border wanted to move towards unity, they would have to get rid of it.'

Ivan Cooper, SDLP member (14 October 1974).

'The terrorists themselves draw support and sustenance from having access to radio and television. The Government has decided that the time has come to deny this easy platform to those who use it to propagate terrorism.'

Douglas Hurd, announcing a broadcasting ban on Irish Republicans (19 October 1988).

'The country is banjaxed. We should hand it back to the Queen in the morning, with an apology.'

Gay Byrne (attrib.), in a remark made on his morning radio show.

'If you can have an exaltation of larks (or a fluff of radio announcers), this was a constipation of a *Late Late Show*.'

Gay Byrne, *The Time of My Life* (1989).

'The radio was only available to us on major sporting occasions like the All-Ireland finals, Mairtín Thornton's fights and de Valera's reply to Churchill.'

Breandán Ó hEithir, *Over the Bar* (1985).

Unparliamentary Language

It's amazing how a swear word can have the desired effect in the right circumstances. Politicians are useless at recognising the right circumstances.

'How do you like that, you bastards? Now you know what it's like in Belfast.'

James Anthony Roche, throwing two canisters of CS gas into chamber of the House of Commons from the public gallery (23 July 1970).

'In my day if a Guard said fuck off you fucked off as quick as you could.'

Charles J. Haughey, in an interview with John Waters, *Hot Press* (29 November 1984).

'If there had not been sufficient wheat fields for Deputy Dillon to die in comfort in any parish in the country before the war, a lot of people during the war would have died in grass fields. If he thinks that camel dung is a better fuel than turf, he may burn it if he likes. I wish to goodness that ostrich feathers were good fuel as, judging by the way he sticks his head in the sand and waves his feathers around, they are easily grown down around Ballaghaderreen.'

Frank Aiken (16 May 1946).

'I mean that, for the record. It's crap, total crap.'

Albert Reynolds (4 November 1992).

'It's been accepted policy and practice, no one said anything about it for fifty years and I'm not going to take the crap for what went on for fifty years.'

Micheál Martin (16 December 2004).

'He chewed the bollix off me and I tore some lumps out of him.'

Albert Reynolds, on John Major's attempt during a meeting on 3 December 1993 to substitute an agreed framework document with a new British one to buy more time, quoted in Fergus Finlay, *Snakes and Ladders* (1998).

'Albert readily accepted my suggestion that we should start the summit with an entirely private meeting. The two of us went into an ornate drawing room in the castle, leaving Paddy Mayhew, Dick Spring and two large delegations to talk elsewhere, and had the frankest and fiercest exchange I had with any fellow leader in my six and a half years as prime minister.'

John Major, *The Autobiography* (1999).

'I am willing to withdraw any remark made by me that casts any reflection on Deputy O'Sullivan's ancestors.'
Seán Lemass (9 May 1929).

'I wish to apologise and ask that the phrase shitehawk be struck from the records, and replace it instead with dirtbird.'
Brian Lenihan (attrib.).

'Do you think you can come here like so many little tin-pot czars, despising the people, showing your contempt for deputies and trampling on Parliament itself? The greatest disservice that was ever done to this parliament was when ministers adopted the phraseology: not in the public interest. If Parliament is not a place where questions can be put and where questions will be answered fully, freely, frankly, then discussion will take place outside and the mischief-maker will enter into the discussions. Every phrase and every phase of life will be distorted and the object inside and behind these discussions will be to tear down. Do you not know that you are breeding revolutionaries by that style of answer like blue-bottles on a dungheap?'
Tom O'Higgins (12 March 1941).

'Two weeks ago the 'in'-word was sleaze while this week it is accountability. If you will excuse my vulgarity, a Cheann Comhairle, it is a lot of bullshit.'
Austin Deasy (27 November 1994).

'The Deputy is a phoney and a fraud. He is a political dirtbird, a political seagull.'
David Andrews (17 November 1983).

'I have been representing a good portion of Cork and a good portion of the present constituency of Cork city for a long number of years and I have seen some of those opposite brought in out of the dung heap and disappearing again pretty quickly.'

Martin Corry (13 November 1963).

'In the midst of the most romantic conversations, conducted on the telephone line, you are likely to have a male voice introduced to know if someone had taken the dung out of the wagon that was on the siding yesterday.'

James Dillon (6 November 1946).

'You cannot expect flowers to grow on dung heaps. In fact, that is what you have in Dublin, dung heaps on which people are living.'

Seán Lemass (20 March 1929).

'Only I had promised Garret that all I was going to do was sit and listen, I'd have been dug out of that bastard.'

Alan Dukes, describing a meeting with an unnamed Catholic bishop about marriage laws (24 August 1989).

'Would you ever fuck off.'

Mary Coughlan, Agriculture Minister to a Meath farmer (March 2005).

'The Assembly is becoming a place where parliamentary immunity is availed of to license slander and where the coarse tongue of a corner-boy can precipitate a brawl, with but the weakest of intervention from the Chair.'

Seán MacEntee, *Irish Press* (28 April 1947).

Richard Anthony: 'One of the Minister's own followers compared this House to a circus.'

A Deputy: 'And now we have the clown.'

Richard Anthony: 'Yes, and the baboon on the other side, the lowest type of mammal.'

Debate on the Wearing of Uniform Restriction Bill (1 March 1934).

'Deputy Fitzgerald has proved his complete inability to represent one constituency by the fact that he has had to jump into another.'

Dan Corry (4 May 1934).

James Dillon: 'Let me at him – hold me back!'

Patrick Smith: 'It is scum, more likely Deputy McGilligan's scum.'

Patrick McGilligan: 'Those parliamentary expressions are good.

Exchange in Dáil Éireann (6 December 1934).

'Shut your mouth and the air will be purer.'

Eamon de Valera, speaking in Dáil Éireann (22 March 1934).

Austin Deasy: 'If you will excuse my vulgarity, a Ceann Comhairle, it is a lot of bullshit. There is no other way to describe it. We have not been told where the information came from.'

Liam Fitzgerald: 'The Deputy has used unparliamentary language.'

Austin Deasy: 'It is much better parliamentary language than

I have heard lately. It is more to the point and does not circumvent the issue.'
Dáil Éireann (22 November 1994).

'Some street corners are better conducted than the way you conduct this House.'
Paddy Harte, to the Ceann Comhairle (14 December 1972).

'The Minister came in here as a senior minister and we were entitled to hear from him a defence of this Bill but we got no defence of this Bill from him. Instead, we got a guttersnipe's speech, a speech worthy of a street corner-boy, and it was sickening to listen to him. It was sad to sit here and to feel that a senior member of the Cabinet could lower himself to make such an irrelevant speech on such a very serious occasion.'
Eddie Collins (1 December 1972).

'I say the Deputy should be removed out of the House. I will put him out – quick, the corner-boy. If he does not shut his – mouth we will shut it for him.'
Andrew Fogarty (17 July 1941).

James Dillon: 'That is the type of base, miserable fraud that characterises Deputy Cogan in this House. He thinks to get away with that slingeing corner-boy quotation and he would have got away with it only that I know him so well.'

Dan Corry: 'On a point of order. Is it in order for a Deputy to call another Deputy a corner-boy?'

An Ceann Comhairle Frank Fahy: 'No, it is not.'

Dan Corry: 'I would ask that the Minister be called upon to withdraw that.'

An Ceann Comhairle Frank Fahy. 'The Minister did not use the term. He said it was a corner-boy quotation.'

Dan Corry. 'I only wished to have the matter established for future reference.'

Dáil Éireann (14 February 1951).

James Dillon. 'That is what the Deputy hopes, but his poisonous and vicious desires to see his neighbours injured in order to bring political grist to his own disgusting mill are usually frustrated. It is not the first generation in which a Moran has sought to see his neighbours suffer that his fortunes might thereby be inflated, and not the first generation which will see that the Moran fortunes are not suffered to batten on the sufferings of their neighbours.'

Michael Moran. 'Every countrywoman knows that you are the fowl pest.'

James Dillon. 'Our people always had the means to protect themselves from the Morans of this country in the past and they will have them in the future, and the Deputy should not reveal his desire to see his neighbour suffer.'

Michael Moran. 'They will want it, so far as the Dillons are concerned.'

Exchange in Dáil Éireann (14 February 1951).

'He is, I believe, the Dr Goebbels of propaganda and the figures I am issuing here today prove conclusively that what he is saying is rubbish.'

Michael McDowell taunting Fine Gael justice spokesman Richard Bruton on garda numbers (March 2006).

Whitehall:

The British Dimension

Being invaded by our neighbouring island was a bit traumatic. Little did we know the trauma was nothing compared with the heavy artillery of words that were to follow.

'England and Ireland may flourish together. The world is large enough for us both. Let it be our care not to make ourselves too little for it.'

Edmund Burke, letter to Samuel Span.

'Now many English of the said land, forsaking the English language, fashion, manner of riding, laws and customs, live and govern themselves by the manners, fashion, and language of the Irish enemies.'

Statutes of Kilkenny (1367).

'I had rather be overrun with a Cavalierish interest than a Scotch interest; I had rather be overrun by a Scotch interest

than an Irish interest, and I think of all this is the most dangerous.'
Oliver Cromwell, speaking to the Council of State (15 March 1649).

'Ludicrous. Ridiculous.'
Collins Concise Dictionary defines the word 'Irish' (1989 edition).

'We British are sometimes told we do not understand the Irish, but if this is so the failure to understand is a two-way street. Everything in which the IRA is currently engaged suggests that it does not understand us at all.'
Peter Brooke, Northern Ireland Secretary of State (6 July 1990).

'Thus you have a starving population, an absentee aristocracy, and an alien Church, and in addition the weakest executive in the world. That is the Irish Question.'
Benjamin Disraeli, speaking in House of Commons (16 February 1844).

'I cannot trace the line of my own future life, but I hope and pray it may not always be where it is. Ireland, Ireland, that cloud in the west, that coming storm, the minister of God's retribution upon cruel and inveterate and but half-atoned injustice.'
W.E. Gladstone, to Mrs Gladstone (1845). Quoted in John Morley, *The Life of William Ewart Gladstone* (1903).

'My mission is to pacify Ireland.'
W.E. Gladstone, on being asked to form a government (1 December 1868).

'Only now by a long, slow, and painful process have we arrived at the conclusion that Ireland is to be dealt with in all respects as a free country, and is to be governed like every other free country according to the sentiments of its majority and not of its minority.'

W.E. Gladstone to Queen Victoria, after the disestablishment of the Irish Church (January 1869).

'This is one of the golden moments of our history – one of those opportunities which may come and may go, but which rarely return or, if they return, return at long intervals.'

W.E. Gladstone, introducing Home Rule Bill (7 June 1886).

'I decided some time ago that if the GOM [Grand Old Man: W.E. Gladstone] went for Home Rule, the Orange Card would be the one to play. Please God it may turn out the ace of trumps and not the two.'

Lord Randolph Churchill to Lord Justice Fitzgibbon (16 February 1886).

'Ireland stands at your bar expectant, hopeful, almost suppliant. Her words are the words of truth and soberness. She asks a blessed oblivion of the past, and in that oblivion our interest is deeper than even hers. My right Hon. Friend, the Member for East Edinburgh [Mr Goschen] asks us tonight to abide by the traditions of which we are the heirs. What traditions? By the Irish traditions? Go into the length and breadth of the world, ransack the literature of all countries, find, if you can, a single voice, a single book . . . . in which the conduct of England towards Ireland is anywhere treated except with profound and bitter condemnation.

Are these the traditions by which we are exhorted to stand?
No; they are a sad exception to the glory of our country.
They are a broad and black blot upon the pages of its
history; and what we want to do is stand by the traditions
of which we are the heirs in all matters except our relations
with Ireland.'

W.E. Gladstone, introducing the first Home Rule Bill, House
of Commons (7 June 1886).

'Ulster at the proper moment will resort to its supreme
arbitrament of force. Ulster will fight, and Ulster will be
right.'

Lord Randolph Churchill, on landing at Larne (22 February
1886).

'Gladstone reserved for his closing days a conspiracy against
the honour of Britain and the welfare of Ireland more
startlingly base and nefarious than any of those other
numerous designs and plots which, during the last quarter of
a century, have occupied his imagination . . . [His] design for
the separation of Ireland from Britain, this insane recurrence
to heptarchical arrangements, this trafficking with treason,
this condonation of crime, this exaltation of the disloyal, this
abasement of the legal, this desertion of our Protestant co-
religionists, this monstrous mixture of imbecility,
extravagance and hysterics . . . this farrago of superlative
nonsense . . . [were such as] the combined genius of Bedlam
and Colney Hatch would strive in vain to produce . . . . [And
why?] For this reason and no other: to gratify the ambition of
an old man in a hurry!'

Randolph Churchill, to the electors of Paddington (June 1886).

'The somewhat mouldy programmes which have crushed the Liberal Party in the past.'

Lord Roseberry repudiating Home Rule in a speech in Liverpool (14 February 1902).

'The old bother about Tyrone and those infernal snippets of Fermanagh and Derry, etc., popped up again.'

Herbert Asquith (21 August 1914). Quoted in Denis Gwynn, *The Life of John Redmond* (1932).

'The Irish on both sides are giving me a lot of trouble just at a difficult moment. I sometimes wish we could submerge the whole lot of them and their island for say ten years under the waves of the Atlantic.'

Herbert Asquith (September 1914). Quoted in Jonathan Bardon, *A History of Ulster* (1992).

'For God's sake bring me a large Scotch. What a bloody awful country!'

Reginald Maudling, British Home Secretary, on a flight back to London after his first visit to Northern Ireland (1 July 1970).

'If men of moderation have nothing to hope for, men of violence will have something to shoot for.'

Harold Wilson (25 November 1971).

'People on this side of the water see property destroyed by evil violence and are asked the bill for rebuilding it. Yet people who benefit from all this now viciously defy Westminster, purporting to act as though they were an elected government; people who spend their lives sponging on

Westminster and British democracy and then system-atically assault democratic methods. Who do these people think they are?'

Harold Wilson, during the Unionist strike which brought down the Sunningdale power-sharing agreement (25 May 1974).

'It is a part of our country, our United Kingdom. Let the people of Ulster be assured of this – the Conservative Party stands rock firm for the Union of Great Britain and Northern Ireland.'

Margaret Thatcher (14 October 1977).

'We are squeezing the terrorists like rolling up a toothpaste tube.'

Roy Mason (4 December 1977).

'I have made it quite clear . . . that a unified Ireland was one solution. That is out. A second solution was confederation of the two states. That is out. A third solution was joint authority. That is out.'

Margaret Thatcher, British Prime Minister, at televised press conference in London (19 November 1984).

'The search for a solution is part of the problem.'

John Biggs-Davison (24 November 1984).

'The Orange card will no longer be a trump card.'

Merlyn Rees (18 November 1985).

'The Northern Ireland Office is always regarded as the dustbin.'

James Prior, former Secretary of State for Northern Ireland (2 September 1985).

'More money for these people? Look at their schools. Look at their roads. Why should they have more money? I need that money for my people in England who don't have anything like this.'

Margaret Thatcher, replying to Garret FitzGerald's suggestion of a joint approach to Europe for additional funding for the International Fund for Ireland (15 November 1985). Quoted in Garret FitzGerald, *All in a Life* (1991).

'I confess that I have always found the Irish, all of them, extremely difficult to understand.'

Edward Heath (27 November 1985).

'We shouldn't have all these campaigns to get the Birmingham Six released. If they had been hanged they would have been forgotten . . . the whole community would have been satisfied.'

Lord Denning (17 August 1990).

'I suspect that the only things that will take out the Irish Constitution is when the bombs begin to blow in Dublin.'

Norman Tebbit, former Conservative minister (1993).

'Britain's interests abroad will be represented by a redundant, second-rate politician from a country peopled by peasants, priests and pixies.'

Robert Kilroy-Silk, right-wing MP, talking about Ray MacSharry (9 November 1992).

'The Irish exploit Britain's welfare state as a kind of patriotic duty.'

Paul Johnson, *Daily Mail* columnist (1994).

'The fucking Irish should learn to live in peace and bloody well get on with it.'

Neville Sanders, Tory leader of Peterborough Council, replying to a request for a twinning arrangement with Carrickfergus council.

'Down through the centuries, Ireland and Britain have inflicted too much pain, each on the other ... We have both grown up now. A new generation is in power in each country.'

Tony Blair (26 November 1998).

'You get more sense from the policeman at the door than from Members of Parliament, and you learn more from him about how to work the system.'

Bernadette Devlin, *The Price of My Soul* (1969).

'All I did was give some money for the buying of more barbed wire: probably parliamentary salary has never been better spent.'

Bernadette Devlin, *The Price of My Soul* (1969).

Women, Suffragettes
and Glass Ceilings

The fair sex had their own wars to fight, in the front line, on the barricades, in the home and in the workplace. No wonder they could be as unfair as anyone else when it came to the crunch.

'The State recognises the Family as the natural primary and fundamental unit group of Society, and as a moral institution possessing inalienable and imprescriptible rights, antecedent and superior to all positive law. The State, therefore, guarantees to protect the Family in its constitution and authority, as the necessary basis of social order and as indispensable to the welfare of the Nation and the State.'

Article 41, the Constitution of Ireland (1937).

'The women of Ireland are very comely creatures, tall, slender and upright. Of complexion very fayre (but freckled) with tresses of bright yellow hayre, which they chain up in curious knots and devises.'

Justice Luke Gernon, 'Discourse' in *Stowe Papers* (1620).

'In particular, the State recognises that by her life within the home – woman gives to the State a support without which the common good cannot be achieved.'

Article 41.21, the Constitution of Ireland (1937).

'I was amazed and disgusted to learn that I was classed among criminals, infants and lunatics – in fact, that my status as a woman was worse than any of these.'

Hanna Sheehy-Skeffington (1900).

'All of us know that Irish women are the most virtuous in the world no country is so faithful to the marriage bond.'

Arthur Griffith (17 October 1903).

'The first step on the road to freedom is to realise ourselves as Irishwomen – not as Irish or merely as women, but as Irishwomen doubly enslaved and with a double battle to fight.'

Constance Markiewicz (1 July 1909).

'Women's suffrage will, I believe, be the ruin of our western civilisation. It will destroy the home, challenging the headship of man laid down by God. It may come in your time, I hope not in mine.'

John Dillon (attrib.) (c.1912).

'Up With Petticoats, Down With Trousers.'

Suffragette slogan in Sandymount (1913). Quoted by Sydney Bernard Smith in *The Irish Times* (23 November 2002).

'The worker is the slave of the capitalist society, the female worker is the slave of that slave.'

James Connolly, *The Reconquest of Ireland* (1915).

'I am not a collector of old fossils.'

Liam Cosgrave, on the jail protest by Maud Gonne MacBride and Constance Markiewicz.

'[There is in Ireland] a regular wave of destruction . . . led by a few ferocious and home-breaking old harridans.'

Oliver St John Gogarty (1 February 1924).

'There is bound to be comment and a degree of unhealthy curiosity in mixed schools and even in schools for girls only, during the latter months of pregnancy of married women teachers.'

Department of Education, memo to Cabinet on why women teachers must retire on marriage (14 February 1953). Quoted in Dermot Keogh, *Twentieth-Century Ireland* (1994).

'We shall not conceive.'

Sung to tune of 'We shall overcome'. Irish Women's Liberation Movement, as they invaded Dáil Éireann through the window of the men's lavatory to promote legalisation of contraception (5 April 1971).

'There are no illegitimate children, only illegitimate parents, if the term is to be used at all.'

Bernadette Devlin, Independent MP for Mid-Ulster and unmarried mother (2 July 1971).

'There is menstrual blood on the walls of Armagh prison.'

Nell McCafferty (1977).

'Any woman voting for divorce would be like a turkey voting for Christmas.'

Alice Glenn (14 May 1986).

'We are now in a position to identify those who can clearly be classified as enemies of the people these would be most of the political parties, the media, spokesmen for the trade unions the Council for the Status of Women, all of the radical feminist organisations, the leadership of most of the Churches, apart from the Catholic Church.'

Alice Glenn (28 November 1986).

'Quite a few male commentators are throwing cold water on the idea of the women's vote but it is there and things will never be the same again.'

Monica Barnes (29 December 1990).

'Women who object to beauty contests are usually ugly. Men who object to beauty contests are usually married to ugly women.'

Krish Naidoo, organiser of Miss Ireland Contest (19 February 1993).

'Trying to end prostitution by criminalising the prostitutes is like trying to end poverty by making it criminal to be poor.'

Mary Harney, speaking on Bill decriminalising homosexual acts (26 June 1993).

'There's women for you.'

Mary O'Rourke, Deputy Fianna Fáil Leader, after Michelle Smith-de Bruin won three gold medals at the Atlanta Olympics (26 july 1996)

'There is a vital place beyond the work place; many women choose to be there. They should be applauded and acknowledged.'

Finola Bruton, wife of Taoiseach John Bruton (1 December 1995).

'A little slogan formed itself in my mind, a cry to the women of Ireland: "More petting, less politics."'

Oliver St John Gogarty, *As I Was Going Down Sackville Street* (1937).

Index